Meditation is a word that is widely respected, used as well as misunderstood and misused. People have some vague notions of meditation but hardly know exactly what it is. This book is for all such people so that they know how simple real meditation is! The real meditation is done with your regular routine. Only the escapists go away to some places or take out special time in the name of meditation!

# Books by Same Author (Dr. Rekhaa Kale)

## Easy Guide to Relationship Building

This book handles all kinds of relations that a person develops. Each relationship that a person comes across in his life span will found in this book and the readers will also get the ways to handle them effectively. Along with discussing the relations, this book also gives tips to build healthy relations. The speciality of this book is that it shows the stumbling blocks in relationships and suggests the ways to handle these blocks effectively.

## Easy Guide to Peace of Mind

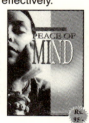

In order to make your mind peaceful, you need to know and understand all the aspects of the mind and the ways in which the mind works. This is because of the universal rule—"A healthy mind stays in a healthy body". This means the health of mind and body are so closely linked that these two are, in fact, just like the two sides of a coin. They are inseparable and exert total influence on each other at all the times in all beings.

## Easy Guide to Feng Shui

Feng Shui, like Indian Vaastu Shastra, believes that the directions play an important role in the luck of an individual. Each direction represents a certain aspiration. It also represents a certain element. This means that when the elements in each direction are in perfect balance, the place has the potential to produce the best luck for the persons staying there. In addition to the directions, Feng Shui also gives a special importance to the various positions in the house irrespective of the direction.

## Easy Guide to Reiki

This book contains levelwise total discussion of Reiki except attunement. Find the original manuals of Reiki by Dr. Usui and Dr. Hayashi in this book. This is one of the few Reiki books that also discuss physiology for a layman. This book is ideal to be used as a standard study material by Reiki teachers. Unlike books on such subjects find maximum summary minimum comments.

## Easy Guide to Dowsing

Dowsing is known to many, but Reiki Dowsing is a unique way to use dowsing. You can learn here that you can heal any ailment by dowsing for the first time. Know about almost all known methods of dowsing and the ways to use them. Find lucid charts of dowsing and use them to scan as well as heal your patient. Find the most user-friendly tips on Reiki Dowsing right from its founder's pen.

---

### Fusion Books

X-30, Okhla Industrial Area, Phase-II, New Delhi-110020, Ph.: 41611861, Fax: 41611861,
E-mail: sales@diamondpublication.com, Website: www.diamondpublication.com

# Easy Guide To
# MEDITATION

Dr. Rekhaa Kale

 **FUSION BOOKS**

**ISBN : 81-89605-86-0**

© Author

**Published by** : **Fusion Books**
              X-30, Okhla Industrial Area, Phase-II
              New Delhi-110020
Phone        : 011-41611861
Fax          : 011-41611866
E-mail       : sales@dpb.in
Website      : www.dpb.in
Edition      : 2007
**Printed by**  : Adarsh Printers, Delhi-110032

**EASY GUIDE TO MEDITATION**
By - *Dr. Rekhaa Kale*                       Rs. 95/-

# INTRODUCTION

Meditation is a word that is widely respected, used as well as misunderstood and misused. People have some vague notions of meditation but hardly know exactly what it is.

Here is a modest attempt to simplify the concept of meditation for the common man so that more and more people can follow the real meditation, and come near real spirituality.

Whenever we think of meditation we think of concentration, stillness, imagination, visualization, postures, crystals, closing eyes, sitting with spine straight and so on and so forth.

All this appears to be quite boring to many. Then these people keep away from meditation. This book is for all such people so that they know how simple real meditation is!

In simple words I shall say that intense concentration in anything leads to meditation. So, even those who work with full sincerity are actually meditating. The real meditation is done with your regular routine. Only the escapists go away to some places or take out special time in the name of meditation!

# CONTENTS

1. Meditation Defined ..... 9
2. Need for Meditation ..... 13
3. Illusion of Meditation ..... 15
4. Resistance of People to Meditation ..... 17
5. Doing Meditation ..... 19
6. Happening of Meditation ..... 22
7. Benefits of Meditation ..... 26
8. Stress Release and Meditation ..... 28
9. Clairvoyance and Meditation ..... 34
10. Success in Life and Meditation ..... 36
11. Failure and Meditation ..... 38
12. Spirituality and Meditation ..... 41
13. Health and Meditation ..... 42
14. Wealth and Meditation ..... 43
15. Well-being and Meditation ..... 44
16. Sex and Meditation ..... 45
17. Yoga, Asana and Meditation ..... 46
18. Tools for Meditation ..... 51
19. Dynamic Meditation ..... 52
20. Inner Gratitude ..... 53
21. Grounding ..... 54
22. Rising ..... 55
23. Rooting ..... 56
24. Unification of Chakras ..... 58

| 25. | Centring | ..... | 60 |
| 26. | Witnessing | ..... | 62 |
| 27. | Energy Circulation | ..... | 63 |
| 28. | Vipaasana Meditation | ..... | 64 |
| 29. | Crystal Meditation (1) | ..... | 65 |
| 30. | Crystal Meditation (2) | ..... | 66 |
| 31. | Kundalini Meditation | ..... | 67 |
| 32. | Naadabrahma Meditation | ..... | 68 |
| 33. | Chakra Meditation | ..... | 70 |
| 34. | Mirror Exercise | ..... | 71 |
| 35. | Jyoti Tratak | ..... | 72 |
| 36. | Developing Your Own Meditation | ..... | 73 |
| 37. | Coming Out of the Doing Trap | ..... | 75 |
| 38. | Imagination, Visualization etc. | ..... | 77 |
| 39. | Kriyas in Meditation | ..... | 85 |
| 40. | Knowing in Meditation | ..... | 87 |
| 41. | Satori and Meditation | ..... | 88 |
| 42. | Doing and Being Meditation | ..... | 92 |
| 43. | Overcoming Escapism | ..... | 97 |
| 44. | Awareness, Enlightenment Beyond | ..... | 103 |
| 45. | Being Meditation in Daily Life | ..... | 110 |
| 46. | Role of Guru in Meditation | ..... | 113 |
| 47. | Role of Silence in Meditation | ..... | 115 |
| 48. | Role of Seclusion in Meditation | ..... | 117 |
| 49. | Role of surroundings in Meditation | ..... | 119 |
| 50. | Role of Chanting in Meditation | ..... | 121 |
| 51. | Role of Posture in Meditation | ..... | 123 |
| 52. | Role of Place in Meditation | ..... | 125 |
| 53. | Role of Knowledge in Meditation | ..... | 127 |
| Appendix | | ..... | 129 |
| Quotes You Can Hang and See Daily | | ..... | 134 |

# 1

# MEDITATION DEFINED

**TO** meditate is to concentrate fully on something and to assimilate it fully with total awareness. The thing to concentrate on may differ from method to method, religion to religion, place to place, discipline to discipline. But the fundamental principle is always the same.

At times, add-ons like postures, breathing control, crystals, essential oils, symbols, incenses, idols or other things like lamps or candles are added to this method. Of course, this is only the additional or extra thing. It does not change the soul of meditation.

Some people are fully engrossed into their work or research. At that time, they are actually meditating. This is because, as per our definition, they are fully concentrating on the thing they are working and are trying to assimilate it fully with total awareness.

Generally, such people are very much practical. They do not believe in the add-ons that come with the methods of meditation. So, they say that they do not believe in meditation and do not even have time for them. They are right. They don't need add-ons; they are anyway meditating on their work!

But, this is not the way in which meditation is widely understood. To a common man, when a person is sitting in a lotus posture, with eyes closed, chanting something or breathing in a particular way, he is meditating! Any other way is not really taken as the real meditation, at least in India! This may be the reason why many think that meditation is a very difficult thing to do!

Real meditation does not need any add-on. It needs only the right mind frame. The mind frame needed for meditation is very much intense, focused such that it has only one centre of awareness and that centre is totally seen, understood, focused, and assimilated by that mind. This centre of focus can be anything. In a famous story of *Mahabharata*, the centre of focus for Arjuna was the fish! Obviously, at that time, Arjuna was meditating very intensely.

I know this definition of meditation may be quite new to others, but those who have been aware of the essence of it would know this.

Such meditation starts unfolding the ways to a seeker on its own! We all know what happened to Eklavya when he just focused on the idol of his master and started practically. In fact, he could get much more and much higher level of knowledge than the best disciple of his master! This was because he was in deep meditation when he was practising!

I have heard a story of a scientist who used to forget everything while working in his lab. He would forget his food too! Once when he was working, his friend came. The scientist did not see him. He was fully engrossed in his experiment. The friend was angry. He finished all the food that was kept for him and went away. When the experiment was successfully completed the scientist realized that he was hungry. He went to have his food. On finding the empty plates, he said to himself, "what a fool I am! I already had eaten the food!" He started working again without realizing the truth about the food! The story will explain about the intense level of meditation he was in.

Meditation makes you forget the whole world and give you the power to create your own world. While intensely meditating, a person may not need even food or water, if the level of his focus is that intense. May be this is the way in which the hermits live without food or water for years in Himalayas!

This level of meditation can give the total feeling of peacefulness, satisfaction, completeness and inner joy. Of course, it also gives lot of power, but the power one gets out of meditation is always gentle, motherly, soft and loving. It lets you govern with love, not with harshness!

This means, when a person is in real total meditation, he is totally free from struggle and stress. Also one has to know that there is never overmeditation. So, those who do their work like meditation are never overworked. They have all the energy to work all the time in all the conditions. Their focus gives them this strength.

This is the real meditation. This means you do not have to take out extra time to be free and do meditation. Meditation is total freedom. It can happen at any time at any place to anyone. Yes, I wrote it could happen! This is because meditation is done by those who want to escape from something. This is just a struggle, struggle leads you nowhere. Meditation is not a tool to let you come out of any trap. It is a beautiful thing like love that happens. When it happens, a person feels fresh, energetic and happy.

There are many who teach meditation like a ritual. May be those who have learned only things like fight and struggle would know only the language of rituals! To bring such people closer to meditation this may prove useful. But, many a time, the seekers as well as teachers get caught in the trap of rituals and the soul of meditation is lost. Then, the whole life, such seekers keep doing meditation without any achievement.

So, one must know that before entering into the field of meditation, one has to know as well as digest the soul of it quite well.

Relaxation and stress release is something that everyone wants, but they try to achieve it by struggling. Struggle cannot get you any relaxation. Meditation is just absence of struggle. When the struggle vanishes, relaxation appears on its own. This happens just like we find that when light appears darkness vanishes on its own.

Meditation is never a doing where one follows some rituals, visualize something, imagine something, concentrate and concentrate by forcibly keeping away other thoughts and then get relaxed and enlightened. Those who say or think that it happens this way are grossly mistaken.

To learn meditation, one must first be ready to unlearn many things like fight and struggle. This means one has to let go our old conditions and rigidity. Then, one is really open to new experience and light of freedom!

# 2

# NEED FOR MEDITATION

**MEDITATION** is needed for all to keep the mind fresh and stress-free. When a person is constantly working and straining himself, there is some thing needed to release the stress that he gathers during this time. It is for this that even a layman needs meditation.

A person also needs meditation to develop his ability of thinking clearly and the ability to comprehend. When a person is meditating regularly, his mind is active in the right way. He does not easily entertain negative thoughts. He also learns to remain calm in the situations that produce anxiety. With the perfect mind, a person can lead a perfect and successful life. This means, meditation is needed to improve the quality of life for a common man.

In addition to this, meditation also has other functions to do. It increases the spiritual level of a person and he starts understanding the real implications behind the prayers. Then he does not blindly believe in God and pray. He knows what he is doing when he is praying. So, his prayer is more like expressing gratitude towards God.

This is how, in short, we can see that meditation is needed by all to improve the normal practical life as well as the spiritual life of everyone. Yet, many do not know the real nature of meditation. So, this book is designed to let all know the real nature of meditation.

# 3

# ILLUSION OF MEDITATION

**WHEN** we sit for meditation, we generally follow some or the other method—we do this step by step. Everytime when we shift from one step to the other we give a suggestion to ourselves that we are relaxing or feeling better. Obviously, the mind takes the suggestions and we feel relaxed. Then we say that we have done successful meditation.

This is good as a relaxation method. But is it really meditation? No, it is not. It is just an illusion of it. The guided meditations or the timed meditations are good for learning the meditation technique. But really speaking they cannot be called meditations. They are just an illusion of meditation.

There are times when we sit to meditate, but the meditation as struggling to meditate we follow all the rituals, but all the time we realize that we were fighting with our mind that was wandering all the time when we were trying to meditate. Catching the mind and forcing it to concentrate on some thought is not meditation! It is an illusion of it.

In short, whenever we find that there is more stress on time, method, concentration, posture etc. we must know that what we are following is an illusion of meditation.

Most of the times, when one is DOING MEDITATION, we must know that, that person is following an illusion of meditation.

This illusion is good enough for relaxing a person, but when it comes to spiritual growth, self-realization and further stages in self-growth, we must remember that illusion of meditation does not take us anywhere. Even if we get some experience like seeing something or seeing some light, or so, we actually need to check if it is a vision or our imagination. At times, we knowingly or unknowingly visualize something or imagine something and then start feeling that it's a vision during our meditation. This is also an illusion of meditation.

## 4

## RESISTANCE OF PEOPLE TO MEDITATION

**THERE** are many people who claim to be practical and so do not believe in meditation. Of course, I do not expect such people to read this book and learn the right ways to meditate. But, I also know that those who are inclined to follow meditation will need to interact with such people at some or other point in their life. It is for these people that I am writing all this.

We need to know that as I have stated at a number of places in this book, the real meditation involves into total confrontation with one's own self. This is the most difficult thing for many people because we do not like to face our own real self. There are many things about it that we do not like. The moment we face this part or our being, we can see how loaded we are and then we automatically start resisting this part of our being. In short, for facing our self we need a lot of courage and not many have this courage. This is the plain and clear reason why many do not like to go to the right way to meditate.

Even when we study the persons who meditate we will find that majority not for knowing their real self or achieving spiritual growth, but for running away from their self and their problems in life.

I must also say one thing very clearly here, that, as of today, the meditation methods are hardly given scientific base. This is the reason why there is a lot of confusion about the nature of meditation and, so, not all understand it rightly.

As a result, some resist it thinking that it is escapism while others keep away from it on knowing that it makes you face yourself.

Those who interpret and express meditation as escapism attract the persons who are looking for some way to run away from themselves. Such people set an example to the logical people to show that meditation is escapism.

Then the logical persons, who do not wish to be put in the category of such escapists, do not even think of getting to know what is meditation and what are its actual benefits. Such people are put off from doing meditation just because of the escapists who create a wrong image of meditation.

This means escapists resist meditation after knowing its real nature because real meditation does not allow any escapism, whereas the logical people, who like to face everything that comes across them straight, resist meditation till they are having an impression that meditation is for escapists. Once they get to know the real nature way they not only accept it, but also follow it well with lot of interest and get maximum benefit out of it. It is seen that only such persons go a long way in spirituality.

# DOING MEDITATION

**LEARNING** meditation is commonly called as learning how to do meditation. When we are doing anything, we are never one with the thing we are doing. The thing done is always different from the one who is doing it.

Those who do meditation need a peaceful undisturbed place, with no noise around. Then they take up their accessories like candles, lamp or incenses, crystals, *yantras* and so on. After this, they sit in the said postures,

concentrate on the said object and struggle to keep away the other thoughts. For this, they, may even keep chanting some *mantra*.

When all this is done with full concentration on rituals for some time, people feel that they have done very good meditation. People keep doing this for days and months and years! Sometimes, they find that something happens to them during this. This is like sudden vibrations in some areas of the body. They feel that these are the experiences due to their intense and regular meditation. They feel very great with this.

Some share these feelings with others proudly as if they got some great blessings from masters. Others just say there are some experiences but our masters have told to keep them as secret because if we speak, we will lose the blessings or powers! By this, they try to show off more!

But in reality what are these experiences? Why do such things as *Kriyas* happen when you are doing meditation? Do they happen even when meditation happens?

Let us see the answers of all these questions:

These experiences or *Kriyas* are just the jerks that one gets as the heavy blocks in certain areas are loosened, hit or released.

The more such experiences one gets, the more it proves that he has lots of rigidity and blocks in his system.

When the energy starts flowing, it hits on the block and is obstructed .

Then there is an inner explosion of energy. This is the

*Kriya*. It is just the process of block release, not an achievement.

The importance given by the seekers to these *Kriyas* is so great that all those are doing meditations.

Wish to experience maximum *Kriyas*. If anyone does not experience any *Kriyas*, he is looked down upon by others in the group who are doing meditation. On the contrary, such a person must be respected and it has to be acknowledged that here is a seeker with least rigidity and blocks. But, such a seeker is given the inferiority feeling and is made to feel that he is going wrong somewhere in doing meditation.

If you are learning to do meditation, it is necessary to keep in mind that the doing part has to be given just the necessary amount of importance. One must never lose the focus from the spirit of meditation on which is the focus itself. The moment you find yourself struggling with anything, catch yourself and stop the struggle. Allow the thought and watch it. Do not hold on to any thought. Do not push away any thought. If necessary get up on catching yourself struggle!

# 6

# HAPPENING OF MEDITATION

**WHEN** you are totally relaxed and are in total surrender to anything that you are doing, you are in meditation. Meditation is happening to you at that time. Then all your stress and struggle just vanish. Your total focus is on the thing you are doing. This need not be any spiritual practice like prayer or worship. It may even be your work that you do for your living or any game that you play to enjoy yourself or any song that you like to sing or any drawing or painting that you are making or any object you are creating or any research you are doing and so on. The list is unending.

You have to understand that meditation happens, instead of struggling to do it. When a child is playing with full concentration on the game, you must have seen that he does not hear the calling of his mother too. He is totally lost in the game. His total focus is on the game. He is just not aware of anything other than the game. This time, the child does not know that he is meditating. When he is doing this, on the contrary, he receives a scolding in not being attentive to Mom's voice! This is how we unlearn the habit of meditation we were born with!

If you like something, how about doing with full focus on it? You can do whatever you are doing fully. Even if you lose awareness of the surrounding for the time being, never mind, because this is the point when actually the real meditation is happening to you! Naturally, if you are doing something out of focus, you would never do with your whole heart. Then your attention is on that thing as well as many other things around, your focus is split and divided into many things and, naturally, the number of inputs your brain receive are also very great then. In such a situation, how can one relax?

When you are totally focused on something, all your energies are flowing to the thing that you are doing. Your mind does not want to go anywhere else as it is very happy where it is. Then there is no running of mind and no pulling it back to focus on something. That means there is no inner struggle. This can happen only to the things you like very much!

But unfortunately, in our society, we find that our hearts' likings are lost in the dos and don'ts that we learn. Our heart has lost the right and permission to express itself fully. If anyone does this, he is called either selfish or shameless! To get social recognition, we have learnt to sacrifice the

voice of our heart. We never know what we paid for the social recognition which still we do not fully get! It is the path to God which we paid as the price to this recognition!

The real learning of meditation is to know who can let it happen. The methods taught in various meditations actually were originally designed to help you let meditation happen. Later on the focus changed. But, the founders of the practices and method cannot be blamed for that!

To let meditation happen, you first have to learn how to look within. We are always aware of what others want or likes but we are hardly aware of what we want or like. We are always concerned about the likes and dislikes, desires and needs of others, but we hardly know our own likes and dislikes, desires and needs in the real sense. We are told by all that the noblest way to live is to live for others and the cruellest way is to live for one's own self. We are also taught that to be cruel is bad.

We don't want to be bad, so we start living for others. Then we lose touch with one's own self. So, it is a good idea to first generate the touch with your own self if you really want to go into meditation.

When you start working to look within yourself, you will realize that you have been doing a number of things that you thought were needed to please others and get you the approval of those persons. But, while doing these things, your heart was never with you. As a result, you would end up in messing up the things you did. The result was that you could neither please that person nor your own heart.

All this has been leaving you in a mess. Then you go on gathering stress and keep struggling to please those whose approvals you think you need very badly in order to have yourself esteemed. This is because you have learned that you are good only when others say so!

While you are in this trap, meditation is very difficult to happen. So, to let meditation happen, you have to come out of this vicious trap, looking within your mind and analyzing all the thoughts very ruthlessly is enough.

Here, I just want to bring one thing to your notice: those who are poor achievers are very much concerned with the social approval, while the social approval and recognition automatically comes to those who excel in some or the other areas in life! So, the best part of getting social approval is making some achievement!

Once you too are looking within yourself, select the thing you always wanted to achieve but had lost in the mess of approval. Start thinking in order to reach your desired goal in the present setup in the best possible way. Of course, for this, you may first have to define your goal. As you start doing this, you will find that your mind has almost stopped struggling!

Now, you are ready to let meditation happen: Pick up any method that you like and follow it. As you start, you will find that mist around your thoughts has started reducing and a right path towards your goal is getting unfolded on its own!

If you find that during the course of meditation the things around are automatically changing in such a way that you are brought nearer to the thing that you always wanted, you will naturally want to surrender to the energies of the divine that you get in touch with during meditation.

In every prayer or worship you are asked to surrender. In fact, the surrender that is thought there cannot be learned. It has to emerge from within. It has to be the same as the surrender for his mother. A total surrender with no resistance! It can only emerge in the above manner that

*Easy Guide to* MEDITATION 25

## 7

# BENEFITS OF MEDITATION

**EVERYTHING** done by everyone is always and necessarily for some benefit. Right now, you are reading this book for some benefit too! Then, what is the problem in knowing the benefits you will get out of meditation? Let us see these benefits:

Those who know how to allow meditation to happen know how to remain relaxed in all situations and how to overcome the anxiety even if it appears in some situation.

These people have a much higher level of concentration and can focus on anything much better.

They have a greater ability to remember, and do not have to struggle for memorizing things.

Their ability of comprehension is much higher than others. This is because they can understand the crux of everything that they come across, learn, read or experience.

These people are much more practical than the other so-called materialist persons. This statement may seem contradictory to those who still have the same old concepts of meditation that the escapist community has instilled in the masses. The real meditation allows you to see the life fully and deal with it with full strength. This makes a person perfectly practical.

These people are able to face and handle any situation

whatsoever. Even if they are escaping a situation at any particular time, they are doing so consciously in order to prepare for the right time. This means the persons who know how to let meditation happen become brave enough to accept, face and handle any situation in life.

These people develop an absolutely positive attitude towards everything in life. They can have gratitude as a part of their being, as they know how to find and get the benefit out of every experience whatsoever.

Meditation also gives you a very solid grounding. This means you remain centred and balanced in every situation whatsoever and handle it well.

In fact this is the ability one always wants to have. We all know that those who can remain strong like a rock when needed can succeed in life in the real sense.

Those who meditate develop this ability. They can handle any situation quite effectively and come successfully out of any situation.

Regular meditations start expanding your aura. Due to this, your ability to connect with the divine starts increasing. Then you are able to know many things like the events that are likely to happen in the future or even the thoughts in the mind of a person with whom you are talking.

Real meditation can give you the experience like self-realization and enlightenment.

Meditation can take you closer to God within. With this you can understand the real meaning of the religion you follow. At a certain point, you may even attain liberation.

## 8

## STRESS RELEASE AND MEDITATION

**AS** we have seen earlier, meditation helps stress release quite effectively. Let us now see how we can actually use meditation for stress release.

When you are stressed waiting to be done, the work is still waiting to be done, you cannot afford a break for a mediation session. This is the time when you really need to know what to do. Many a time a person runs to meditation in such a situation because he wants to escape the stress;

this multiplies the stress. One cannot meditate properly because one is not relaxed and one cannot relax because one cannot meditate. In this process, lot of time is lost and the stress multiplies further because only a little time is left to finish the work.

Since many who try to meditate in order to be free from stress have this experience, people are put off from approaching meditation even if they are stressed out. Then people just say that meditation is waste of time. Those who have nothing to do go in for meditation. If a person does not do anything because he meditates, how can he have stress anyway?

These are common conversations about meditation. But I will not blame those who say so though I am writing here about meditation. The reason is, without proper knowledge of how one can simply get into meditation and do the work the moment one finds that he is stressed, one has to feel all this and there is nothing wrong in it.

But, once a person knows how to meditate while working, he will never ever say that meditation is escapism or waste of time!

To get into meditation on feeling stress is very simple.

Be where you are. You may even keep the eyes open. Touch the tip of the tongue to upper pallet. Just concentrate on your breath: as you can concentrate on the breathing watch the path of air going in and coming out. Slowly increase the depth of your breaths. When you do this, you will feel that your body is relaxed. Now, feel the energy from the base of your spine and perineum rising up slowly. Feel this energy going up your crown centre and then coming down and settling at your third eye. This will not only relax you but also help you get more focused at the thing you are working on. Moreover, you can do all this without spending any extra time, while you are still working on the problem or situation.

This is a simple process that helps you relax when you have no time to relax or rest. Such a meditation is certainly not waste of time or escapism. It is also not inactivity because a person is doing it very much, while doing one's work.

When you are using meditation for stress release in general times, you need to know that stress is caused by some specific reasons and that these reasons must be first understood before you actually work out to have it. If you use only one standard type of stress, you may find that sometime the stress is released, but at other times the stress is multiplied instead of getting released. Then you say that meditation is not the right tool for handling stress. But, hardly anyone understands that it is not the fault of meditation. It is the fault of the method you follow.

I would recommend that in the beginning follow the method I have already given to handle the sharpness of stress. Then, take some time to look into the cause of your stress. Check for the things, events, persons, thoughts or experiences that you are resisting. Look into the reason of resistance. See the fear involved with the resistance. Check the possibilities and level of harm that may be caused to you if the resisted thing materializes. See if there is any way to handle this harm. Now, again look into your mind and check the resistance level. Check if your preparation to handle the harm. Again, look into your mind and check the resistance level. Check if your preparation to handle this unwanted thing, event, person or experience is totally complete. If you see any incompletion, take time and care to complete them. Once you are sure that now even if this unwanted thing happens, you will be able to bear and handle the harm without much major loss, and start working on the stress about this thing in your mind.

In fact as you do all this most of the stress will have gone by the end of this work.

Yet, there is some stress left and the traces of the past stress that are reflecting into the body are left too. Now, use meditation to handle this. This will release all the remaining stress, tension and fatigue.

The meditation needed at this point is very simple, but cannot be rightly practical unless and until all the above steps are properly done. If you start with the meditation without these steps, two things will happen. Firstly, you will end up in running away from the stress-producing thing, event or person and secondly, this escapism ends up in worsening the situation and as a result even during the time of doing meditation, one feels good; after some time one finds oneself in a greater mess and then repents for doing the meditation going into illusion and running away from the truth! In fact, most of the people never even realize this and keep on going on and on. This is the reason why people generally look down upon those who claim to use meditation for handling their problems and stress. If you don't use the right way, these reactions are justified too!

So, on finding that stress is building up, before it breaks down, do follow the steps that are given above. Now, when it comes to handling the left out stress after the cause and inability to handle the situation is well handled, do this:

- ❖ Sit in a comfortable position.
- ❖ Close your eyes.
- ❖ Focus on the part of your body where you find

stress.

- ❖ As you breathe, try to breathe through this stressed out area of your body.
- ❖ As you breathe in, breathe relaxation in for the stressed tense area.
- ❖ As you breathe out, breathe out tension, pressure, stress and resistance from your system.
- ❖ Do the above processes for about ten minutes and feel the stress going out of your system totally.
- ❖ When you feel fully relaxed, open your eyes.
- ❖ Now think of the same thing that was giving stress, with full intensity as if you are about to start that activity or have that experience.
- ❖ Watch your own reaction to the situation now.
- ❖ If you find that the same thought is being received by being fully at ease, know that you are on the right track.
- ❖ If you feel the same or almost the same restlessness, know that whatever you had done till now in the name of working on the problem was just a plain waste of time. Know that you were just trying to cheat yourself and so go back to that step and work again.
- ❖ When this stage is clear, you can move ahead to ensure that the stress won't come back again.
- ❖ At this stage, practise focusing on your third eye.

- ❖ When you can do this well, simply try to breathe light in with your third eye as you breathe in air in normal way.

- ❖ Let the light taken in spread all over your head.

- ❖ Let all the darkness, confusion, pressures, tension, struggle, anger, etc. vanish as the light spreads into your head and let your head feel lighter, wiser and happier.

- ❖ Now, watch yourself thinking over the issues that you would find difficult to handle.

- ❖ If you feel the same stressful and struggling reaction, it means you need to repeat the exercise for a longer time.

- ❖ When you find that thinking over the problem or issue does not make you tense any more, know that you have succeeded in handling stress with meditation.

This is a sure and certain method of handling stress with the help of meditation.

If this method that actually contains a perfect combination of meditation, introspection and logical reasoning is rightly followed, one can certainly say that meditation can help in the right way to handle stress.

## CLAIRVOYANCE AND MEDITATION

**CLAIRVOYANCE** is seeing something that the normal people do not see. There is a very thin line of difference between hallucination and clairvoyance. Hallucination is the creation of conscious or subconscious imagination. It has no connection with reality. On the other hand, clairvoyance is the process of seeing or hearing the things that are not seen or heard by normal persons and these seen or heard things are real. Their reality is proved over a period of time when the things seen or heard are seen to come true.

Very few people have this ability. They are called psychic. Some people are born psychic; some develop it in the course of meditations.

When you meditate you get connected with the inner self with that universal consciousness that has all the knowledge and information in store. When this connection happens one can get to know many things that are not known to the normal mind. Then the people with normal mind call these people as psychic and say that they have some special powers.

In fact, the more you meditate the stronger are your connections with the inner self. With the stronger inner self, the connection with the universal awareness too gets stronger.

Then as you meditate, you automatically get to know about many things that are about to happen. These may come as a vision or as a voice message or just something that you feel you know.

Initially, one may not believe that the thing that he has seen or heard is really a clairvoyant experience. But, when more than two or three times he finds that what he had seen has come true, he realizes that he has developed the clairvoyance.

The other aspect of clairvoyance is seeing the aura of a person or seeing energy bodies, soul and energies present in different places and things. With this ability, one can easily find out or feel if the place is good or not, if there is any soul, spirit or angel around in the area and so on and so forth. Also when one can see the aura of a person, one can know about the health condition of the mind and body of that person just by looking at him. This happens with meditation.

※ ※ ※

# 10

## SUCCESS IN LIFE AND MEDITATION

**EVERYONE** in life seeks success. But, those who find it difficult to get it, they get depressed, upset and also restless. Such times they need something that will help them regain their peace of mind.

Meditation is known to be a way to keep the mind peaceful and focused. So, generally people take to meditation when they are stressed out. Of course there is no harm in doing so, but meditation is not only a tool of stress release. It is also a tool to help you get the long awaited success. Don't believe what I say? Then let me explain how it happens:

When you wish to achieve anything very badly but doubt whether you will get it or not, you can try meditation to succeed. See how:

When you are clear about your goal, think of all possible ways to reach, then as you sit or lie down to meditate keep thinking of your goal when you are getting deeper into meditation. This means when you want to meditate for success, watch the goal instead of your thoughts or your breath. Watch your thoughts regarding the goal and watch your inner changes as you meditate over your goal.

When you do this, you will be clearly aware of your inner blocks in reaching your goal and succeeding. Once you are aware of the blocks, you can choose either to work on them or to reset the goal.

If we work on the blocks, as we approach the goal the number of problems that we face are very less and also we are aware of most of the problems and know how to handle them.

If we reset the goal, it is again necessary to meditate over the revised goal to find out our blocks about it. It may so happen that we have not noticed all the blocks before we actually start our goal-directed action. This is physical action and not visualization or imagination. Some think that even the goal-directed behaviour and the success-gaining has to be visualization. But remember you are using meditation as a tool to succeed and not as a tool to do daydreaming. What you are seeking is a good success and not a good dream!

Actually the practical people who are seen to ridicule the concepts are right too. If those who talk about meditating into success are actually talking about imagining of success while sitting in meditation, any practical person is going to laugh at this concept.

The method mentioned above for success involves both meditation and action. Here we use meditation to let us know the problems and blocks in reaching the success and then we actually handle them and act to get success. This is the way any practical person will love to follow.

Also as we are doing all this, it is good idea to check our reactions that may occur in case we face failure. It is seen that at times even these reactions help us detect the blocks in success that we had not seen earlier. So while working for success, if we can come across unexpected problems, we need to follow this exercise of checking our reaction to possible failure and handle the block to success when located. Try it. Best of luck for success!

## 11

# FAILURE AND MEDITATION

**FAILURE** is inability to reach the desired goal. At times failure gives you a chance to reach the goal again in the next attempt, but at other times, we do not get such a chance. So, the kind of failure has to be examined every time when we talk of failure.

The failure that gives the next chance to attempt to succeed is relatively tolerable but the failure that cannot be converted into success is not easily accepted by people.

The emotion that is generally felt after failure is that of frustration or depression. This makes the person sad or angry as the case may be.

People generally do meditation to overcome the depression that they feel after failure. For this, the standard methods are of concentration on breath and breathing out all the depression as well as frustration and breathing in the positive thoughts. But technically speaking this method is only distracting the mind and making it think of something else.

This can soften the edge of your frustration but it will hardly help you to get the best out of whatever you have received in the name of failure. This is the reason why when you face failure, the practical people say that it is a good idea to take some anti-depressant and get on to work instead of wasting your time on meditation. True. When you take an antidepressant tablet you do not have to sit and wait for the result. You can go on doing your work and the medicine does its work!

But meditation done in the appropriate way not only helps you handle the failure, but also shows stepping stone to success.

For using meditation in this way, the first requirement is that we must have a practical attitude. We have to accept the fact that we have failed in the venture at this moment. But we must also realize that this is not the end of the road. So, we can very much work on the situation to succeed if not in this venture, may be in similar future venture. We can also know that this failure has taught us many things that can be used to gain success in future.

Let us see how we must meditate after facing the failure and feeling low after it. It is a good idea to begin with the gratitude exercise.

Once you do the meditation exercise of gratitude that is given in the book along with other methods of meditation, you may feel fresh and light and then you can do the following exercise:

1) Look into your innermost mind for your real reaction to the failure.

2) If you find that you are upset due to something specific, check it carefully and find out whether any part of that reaction leading to upset has a potential to cause that failure.

3) The moment you have the least doubt about this, just focus on the failure and start watching your reactions and your thoughts about it as you meditate.

4) It is advisable to do this part of the exercise while being in Shavasana. This is because here it is likely that you may go very deep in the meditation and arrive at the real causes of failure. So, it is necessary that at no point of time one must get disturbed during meditation.

5) Once you see the real cause, try to look into the matter to find the ways to bypass the cause of failure. Use meditation for this too. When the path is seen follow it in reality.

## 12

# SPIRITUALITY AND MEDITATION

**SPIRITUALITY** is generally taken as the process and path of seeking the real nature of our being and of God.

In fact, the science for a very advanced level seeks the knowledge about the origin of the universe. But when we talk about principles and laws it becomes a science and when we talk about energies and creator, it becomes spirituality.

It is always believed that meditation helps us grow spiritually. The statement is not wrong, but we forget one thing and this is just one thing that we can achieve with meditation out of the many things that we can achieve.

Meditation helps us have our aura expanded, cleaned and well connected with the universal energies. This is actually known as spiritual growth.

With meditation this happens on its own and then with the cleared aura and well developed intuition and good connection with the divine awareness, one can know many things that, at other times, it may be difficult to know. From this point of view we can say that meditation introduces you into real spirituality.

# HEALTH AND MEDITATION

**HEALTH** is determined by the perfect equilibrium of all the systems and all the chemicals in our body. This is maintained with the help of many things like right diet, right habits, right thinking and stress-free mind and body. But it is seen that when people are in meditation regularly, they are healthy even in spite of irregularities in any of the things like diet, habits or stress and rest.

When one meditates or when one is used to be in meditation for all the time in the day, one has a very clean and positive frame of mind. This frame helps to regain the inner balance.

This means when we meditate we normally have a good health, or the methods we follow for meditation are appropriate and we are not using meditation to escape our problems.

As we meditate we internally know the exact kind of imbalance that is within and we can work to set it right.

Remember, meditation does not cure the existing ailments. For that we always need medicine, but the new illness is not created.

**14**

# WEALTH AND MEDITATION

**IF** meditation can help to gain success and handle failure it can also help to gain wealth.

Let us see how this can happen: Remember we need not gain wealth in visualization and dream. It has to happen in reality by using meditation.

To gain wealth what we need is sincere efforts and awareness of ourselves towards wealth gaining.

In fact we find that many times the attitude that we have for wealth is responsible for the wealth that we gain.

At times we feel that we are not worth a lot of wealth. We only deserve to be poor. Then whatever we may try, still we cannot be rich. So, we must first see what image we have of ourselves as far as wealth is concerned. Then work on that image by using meditation as a tool for genuine ruthless introspection. Handle all the blocks and desires to be poor or thoughts that make you feel that you deserve to be poor. Once this is done, you can start working to gain wealth. You are sure to succeed. Try it out!

# 15

# WELL-BEING AND MEDITATION

**SINCE** meditation helps you gain total balance and equilibrium, it has a potential to generate a total well-being within and around. Such a well-being not only includes good health and wealth but also good relations and goodwill that a person carries around.

The person who meditates regularly has the vibrations that are pleasant, positive and peaceful. With these types of vibrations around the person automatically attracts harmony, goodwill, good health and happiness. These are the things that go to create the well-being.

So, automatically meditation gives rise to the well-being around a seeker and in that a person develops the potential to get everything that he really needs in his life to maintain this well-being.

This harmony has no struggle whatsoever and here the right and the good things happen on their own without any conscious efforts of the seeker. The seeker is only in total surrender to the grace as he is in regular intense meditation while he is carrying out all his daily duties and responsibilities.

## 16

# SEX AND MEDITATION

**IT** is commonly believed that when you are doing meditation you must keep away from sex. It is also believed that sex brings hindrance to your spiritual growth, so if you are on a spiritual path, you need to keep away from sex, both in body and mind.

But thinkers like Osho say just the reverse. Osho claims that sex is the best possible way to enter meditation. This statement has also created lot of controversy as it has shattered the existing beliefs completely.

In fact sex is as natural as breathing or eating food. There is nothing right or wrong about it! If there is anything wrong about sex the same is even wrong about eating food, living in a shelter, drinking water, wearing clothes and even breathing.

But we do not consider these things wrong. Yet there is a taboo about sex. This is the reason why the thoughts about it become biggest blocks in meditation. It spoils both the sex and the meditation.

Once we remove these blocks and start being in meditation even during sex, we can see a great shift in meditation.

✳ ✳ ✳

# 17

# YOGA, ASANA AND MEDITATION

Generally, in one Indian setup, meditation is combined with yoga. The reason is that *Samadhi* or meditation has been the final stage in the *Ashtanga Yoga* i.e. eight-fold path of a seeker. *Yoga* means a path of a seeker. We have eight stages of it, namely, *Yama, Niyama, Pranayama, Asana, Pratyahar, Dhyan, Dharana* and *Samadhi*.

The path of meditation starts at *Dhyan* and ends at *Samadhi*.

*Yama* is self control. This is the first quality that a master has to develop. Self control does not mean self restraint.

Self control is having all your controls and strings in your hands. A person with total self control always gets. No one can induce him to react against his own free will. We have always seen that in life we are always interacting with people. During this, we observe that many times, the behaviour of others upsets us. Then we do something that is totally wrong in our own eyes. We repent for them later on.

If you have all your controls with yourself, this won't happen!

It is true that this is not so easy. But unless you so this, you cannot go to the next stage of *yoga*. It is a good idea to check when you lose your controls and at what kinds of acts of others.

Be careful and try to get back your controls whenever you face such situations in future.

When you find that you have all controls with yourself, know that you are now ready to go to the next stage. This is *Niyama*, or regularity. Generally, this stage is mistaken for the set of rules that one has to follow. This is just because *Niyama* also means rule. Discipline is again a word that is grossly misinterpreted. Discipline is called strict following of some set of rules. In fact, discipline is the path towards a goal. This can be followed only when you have a goal and have a strong will to reach that goal. Once you set a goal and plan your path towards it, you have to be consistent in your work. This consistency is actually called *Niyama* in *yoga*. It can come when you are regular and consistent!

Then the stage of *Pranayama* comes. It means breath control in the gross language. In fact, *Prana* is the life force in a person and *yama* is the dimensions. This means we work on the dimensions of a life force when we practise *Pranayama*.

We receive and give away the life force with the breath that we inhale and exhale. The regulation of the inhaling and exhaling as well as the gap between these two can shift your dimensions of life. When you enter a higher life dimension, you can be in touch with many advanced spiritual masters and knowledge. This is the reason why *Pranayama* is given great importance in spiritual path that is followed by many.

*Asana* is the posture. The posture of your sitting, standing or even sleeping has the potential to regulate the energies in your system. The flow of energies that the body gets with each *Asana* is different. Each *Asana* is meant to serve a specific purpose in spirituality as well as in life. But unfortunately, in present common knowledge, *yoga* is just *Asanas*, meant for physical fitness. I must say that physical fitness is absolutely necessary for spiritual growth, but that is the path and not the goal of spirituality.

*Pratyahara* is inner focus with non-attachment. When you are going in the path of spirituality, it is very necessary that you must be free from attachments this is because attachment is something that binds you to things outside and you lose your freedom and focus. When you get total inner focus, you can concentrate on anything that you're doing in any situation whatsoever. Then nothing disturbs you or distracts you, your concentration level goes up and your ability to work too increases considerably as you start practising *Pratyahara*.

This is a vital step before real meditation. The present popular practice of *Vipaasana* is based on this stage of *yoga* and is able to give great breakthrough to the seekers.

*Dhyana* is concentrating on something or object. Once you

have developed *Pratyahara* or focus, you can focus on the object you wish to meditate on. When you intensely concentrate on the object of meditation all your focus shifts from things around and things and thoughts within, and go on the thing you are concentrating on. Then you are fully aware of that object and all the other awareness slowly vanishes. This does not mean you become blind and deaf to the other stimuli. This only means that though your brain receives the other stimuli it does not react to them unless necessary.

This means as we practise *Dhyana*, we automatically know how much importance each stimuli observes and we learn to ignore the things that earlier used to distract us unnecessarily. To those who practise *Dhyana*, these things no more distract any more and one can fully concentrate at will in any situation whatsoever!

*Dharana* is analyzing and assimilating all that which you are concentrating on. When we focus on something totally and intensely, in *Dhyana*, the edge of the other stimuli becomes blunt and the other stimuli no more distracts. So, one can go ahead to assimilate, understand, know and analyse all the aspects of the objects we are focusing on. This is the time we start practising *Dharana*. It allows us to understand the object of focus very thoroughly. This understanding does not happen when somebody helps teach you about that object or show its aspects, properties or qualities. It happens when you see all these things yourself. Then what you have assimilated does not require any memorizing. It automatically becomes a part of your system. This is the reason why those who learn by themselves in analytical way do not have to remember consciously and yet they have a photographic memory. Each of their experiences becomes a part of their system!

*Samadhi* is meditation. This happens when you assimilate all the qualities of the object you are concentrating on. With all its aspects assimilated, you reach the stage when you get into contact with the divine awareness and get to know more about that thing. Here the divine thoughts start reflecting into your minds and then you can comprehend the object quite clearly. All your doubts and questions dissolve and automatically get converted into the solutions, explanations and answers.

*Samadhi* too has a number of levels and textures. When you are lost in your thought, you are in *Bhaava Samadhi*. When you are lost in the thoughts and image of your beloved you are in *Premsamadhi*. When your object of concentration is devoted to God, you are in *Bhaktisamadhi*. When your object of concentration is your work, when you enter *Samadhi*, your *Samadhi* is *Karyasamadhi*.

When you reach the ultimate point in *Samadhi*, which of course only handful of masters could reach till now, your focus becomes so intense that the barriers between life and death too vanishes. Then you can be in that state for as much time as you wish. While in the state of meditation this way, you become so still that even your breathing and heartbeats too stop and every particle of your being is in the state of meditation. The only sign of life in this state is your body temperature that does not fall even if your heart is not beating and your breath is not functioning! These are a few instances of masters and *yogis* going to this state and remaining there for a few days.

Yet the state when practised for longer and longer durations, a person is said to develop the ability of getting converted into life. This happens as each and every cell of his body gets into meditation and is able to touch and merge with the ultimate consciousness. This point is known as *Sanjeevan Samadhi*. Generally when the masters reach this level, they plan to say goodbye to the world and leave the world with body as we hear it!

## 18

# TOOLS FOR MEDITATION

**THOSE** who are still DOING meditation find that the practice becomes better with certain tools. These are candles, incenses, light, crystals, essential oils, chanting, bells, and specific seats and so on.

All these things individually or totally contribute to create the atmosphere where the mind of a person relaxes and a person goes in true *Alfa* state of mind where there is total relaxation and total awareness.

This is the state where real meditation happens.

The tools of meditation are responsible for creating an atmosphere where the mind can get centred into ones own inner self. Then the mind gets so much at peace that we can reach the stage between sleep and waking. This is the *Alfa* state. Even when one is hypnotizing a person or one is using the *Silva* mind control method, one actually brings the mind to this state itself, the only difference being that in the other methods some inputs are given to the mind while in meditation, the divine energies are allowed to put the inputs.

## DYNAMIC MEDITATION

- ❖ Close your eyes and start laughing loudly for 15 minutes.
- ❖ Start crying loudly for 15 minutes.
- ❖ Beat the pillow with hand for 15 minutes.
- ❖ Dance with eyes closed for 15 minutes.
- ❖ Lie down still for 15 minutes.

✻ ✻ ✻

## 20

## INNER GRATITUDE

- ❖ Sit in a comfortable position.
- ❖ Close your eyes.
- ❖ Think of all who helped you.
- ❖ Think of the benefit you got out of the help.
- ❖ Thank them.
- ❖ Think of all those who harmed you.
- ❖ Find the benefit you got thro' that harm.
- ❖ Thank them.
- ❖ Think of those whom you helped.
- ❖ Find the benefit you got out of that help.
- ❖ Thank them.
- ❖ Think of those whom you harmed.
- ❖ Mentally ask forgiveness for the harm you did.
- ❖ Think of benefits both of you got from the harm.
- ❖ Thank them for tolerating you.
- ❖ Think of the natural resources that contributed.
- ❖ Thank them.
- ❖ Feel the gratitude everywhere.
- ❖ Find yourself thankful to all the creations of God.
- ❖ Slowly open your eyes and start your routine.

✳✳✳

## 21

# GROUNDING

- ❖ Sit in a comfortable position.
- ❖ Close your eyes.
- ❖ Concentrate on your breathing.
- ❖ Be aware of the energies around.
- ❖ Be aware of your thoughts.
- ❖ Find the thoughts that make you comfortable.
- ❖ Find the thoughts that make you restless.
- ❖ Know that restlessness is due to non-grounding.
- ❖ Let the divine love shower on you.
- ❖ Let these energies enter thro' top of head.
- ❖ Let these energies fill your body.
- ❖ Feel the comfort with these energies.
- ❖ Let the disturbing thoughts develop roots.
- ❖ Let these roots go into the ground.
- ❖ Request these roots to reach the solution.
- ❖ Feel relief from the upsets.
- ❖ Now let the divine love create total rooting.
- ❖ Feel perfectly grounded with practical attitude.
- ❖ Slowly open your eyes and start the routine.

## 22

## RISING

- ❖ Sit in a comfortable position or lie down.
- ❖ Concentrate on your root centre.
- ❖ Feel a stream of golden light entering here.
- ❖ Feel this stream going upwards to *hara*.
- ❖ Feel this stream going upwards to solar plexus.
- ❖ Feel this stream going upwards to heart.
- ❖ Feel this stream going upwards to throat.
- ❖ Feel this stream going upwards to third eye.
- ❖ Feel this stream going upwards to crown.
- ❖ Feel this stream going out into your whole aura.
- ❖ Feel the *chakras* turning gold and vibrating.
- ❖ Feel the power of the golden energy within you.
- ❖ Open your eyes slowly and start the routine.

## 23

## ROOTING

- ❖ Sit in a comfortable position or lie down.
- ❖ Visualise a stream of white light entering your crown.
- ❖ Visualise the stream of white light filling your crown.
- ❖ Visualise the stream turning it into a glowing white ball.
- ❖ Visualise the stream of white light filling your third eye.
- ❖ Visualise the stream turning it into a glowing white ball.
- ❖ Visualise the stream of white light filling your total head.
- ❖ Visualise the stream turning it into a glowing white ball.
- ❖ Visualise the stream of white light filling your throat.
- ❖ Visualise the stream turning it into a glowing white ball.
- ❖ Visualise the stream of white light filling your chest.
- ❖ Visualise the stream turning it into a glowing white ball.

- Visualise the stream of white light filling your diaphragm.
- Visualise the stream turning it into a glowing white ball.
- Visualise the stream of white light filling your naval.
- Visualise the stream turning it into a glowing white ball.
- Visualise the stream of white light filling your thighs.
- Visualise the stream turning it into a glowing white ball.
- Visualise the stream of white light filling your legs.
- Visualise the stream turning it into a glowing white ball.
- Visualise the stream of white light filling your whole body.
- Visualise it turning your body into a glowing white ball.
- Visualise extra light coming out of hands and foot soles.
- Visualise it going into the ground.
- Feel the entire path of energy clearly and consciously.
- Feel the lightness within you.
- Slowly open your eyes and resume your routine.

❈ ❈ ❈

## 24

## UNIFICATION OF CHAKRAS

- ❖ Sit in a comfortable position or lie down.
- ❖ Concentrate on your heart centre.
- ❖ Visualise your heart centre opening.
- ❖ Visualise a stream of white light entering it.
- ❖ Visualise your heart centre expanding.

- Visualise it covering your throat and solar plexus.
- Visualise your heart centre expanding further.
- Visualise it covering your third eye and *hara*.
- Visualise your heart centre expanding further.
- Visualise it covering your crown and root.
- Visualise your heart centre expanding further.
- Visualise it covering your emotional body and knees.
- Visualise your heart centre expanding further.
- Visualise it covering your mental body and ankles.
- Visualise your heart centre expanding further.
- Visualise it covering your spiritual body and your foot soles.
- Visualise your heart centre expanding further.
- Visualise it covering your whole body.
- Visualise your expanded heart covered by cobalt blue light.
- Visualise your expanded heart covered by dark violet light.
- Visualise your expanded heart covered by golden light.
- Feel yourself full of love and light.
- Slowly open your eyes and start your routine.

✷ ✷ ✷

## 25

## CENTRING

- ❖ Sit in a comfortable position or lie down.
- ❖ Observe the path of your breath.
- ❖ While inhaling, concentrate on the root and count 1.
- ❖ Totally concentrate on exhaling.
- ❖ While inhaling, concentrate on the *hara* and count 2.
- ❖ Totally concentrate on exhaling.
- ❖ While inhaling, concentrate on your S.P. and count 3.
- ❖ Totally concentrate on exhaling.
- ❖ While inhaling, concentrate on heart and count 4.
- ❖ Totally concentrate on exhaling.
- ❖ While inhaling, concentrate on throat and count 5.
- ❖ Totally concentrate on exhaling.
- ❖ While inhaling, concentrate on third eye and count 6.
- ❖ Totally concentrate on exhaling.
- ❖ While inhaling, concentrate on crown and count 7.
- ❖ Totally concentrate on exhaling.

- Now go in the reverse way.
- While inhaling, concentrate on crown and count 7.
- Totally concentrate on exhaling.
- While inhaling, concentrate on third eye and count 6.
- Totally concentrate on exhaling.
- While inhaling, concentrate on throat and count 5.
- Totally concentrate on exhaling.
- While inhaling, concentrate on heart and count 4.
- Totally concentrate on exhaling.
- While inhaling, concentrate on your S.P. and count 3.
- Totally concentrate on exhaling.
- While inhaling, concentrate on the *hara* and count 2.
- Totally concentrate on exhaling.
- While inhaling, concentrate on the root and count 1.
- Totally concentrate on exhaling.
- While inhaling, concentrate on ground and count 0.
- Totally concentrate on exhaling.
- Feel a total peace within.
- Feel yourself firmly grounded.
- Find yourself as a pure witness.
- Open your eyes and start your routine.

✻ ✻ ✻

## 26

## WITNESSING

- ❖ Sit in a comfortable position in front of a mirror.
- ❖ Look at yourself in the mirror.
- ❖ Watch the thoughts that come to your mind.
- ❖ Watch the emotions you feel about yourself.
- ❖ Watch the hatred you feel for yourself.
- ❖ Experience all emotions attached with this feeling
- ❖ Watch the frustrations you feel.
- ❖ Experience all emotions attached with this feeling
- ❖ Watch the disgust you feel about yourself.
- ❖ Experience all emotions attached with this feeling.
- ❖ Watch the insecurities you feel in life.
- ❖ Experience all emotions attached with this feeling.
- ❖ Watch all your inferiorities as you visualise.
- ❖ Experience all emotions attached with this feeling.
- ❖ Watch all the hurts you have gone thro'.
- ❖ Experience all emotions attached with this feeling.
- ❖ Acknowledge all this that your mind contains.
- ❖ Find yourself as a pure witness.
- ❖ Open your eyes and start your routine.

✻ ✻ ✻

## ENERGY CIRCULATION

- Lie down on your back.
- Bend your legs and bring them closer to your hips.
- Close your eyes.
- Visualise a half black and half white ball in the centre of your head.
- Visualise your genitals.
- Visualise their colour changing to dark blue.
- Concentrate in the back of your head.
- See the same dark blue there.
- Find all your extra sexual energies drawn upwards.
- Now you can use the extra sexual energy for creativity.
- Find all your energies in perfect balance.
- Feel a total peace within.
- Feel yourself firmly grounded.
- Find yourself as a pure witness.
- Open your eyes and start your routine.

✻ ✻ ✻

## 28

## VIPAASANA MEDITATION

- ❖ Sit with spine straight.
- ❖ Close your eyes.
- ❖ Concentrate on your breathing.
- ❖ Slowly start shifting your focus within.
- ❖ Slowly find the external stimuli vanishing.
- ❖ Be in this state for about 10 minutes.

✻ ✻ ✻

## 29

# CRYSTAL MEDITATION (1)

- Sit in lotus posture with eyes closed.
- Place eight white crystals around you on eight sides.
- Place Amethyst Pyramid on your crown.
- Place rose quartz pyramid behind root.
- Hold white quartz pyramid in your hand over each other in receiving below naval.
- Sit like this for 10 minutes feeling energy.

✷ ✷ ✷

## CRYSTAL MEDITATION (2)

❖ Mark the area where you will lie down.

❖ Place the crystal above crown area, two crystals at shoulder, two at wrist level, two at knee level and one below feet all above six inches away from the body.

❖ Lie down with eyes closed between these crystals for 20 minutes and feel the energy.

✸ ✸ ✸

## KUNDALINI MEDITATION

- Sit with spine straight.
- Close your eyes.
- Focus on your root and feel the ball of golden energy.
- Watch this ball loosening up and moving up.
- Feel it going into the *hara*.
- Feel it going into the solar plexus.
- Feel it going into the heart.
- Feel it going into the throat.
- Feel it going into the *ajna chakra*.
- Feel the golden ball converted into a chord till crown.
- Feel it coming up, moving out of the crown and connecting to God.
- Stay still and watch this.
- Then slowly find the golden chord coil again.
- Find it forming a golden ball and settling in root *chakra* again.
- Open your eyes and get up.

✳ ✳ ✳

## NAADABRAHMA MEDITATION

- Sit with spine straight and legs folded.
- Concentrate on breathing.
- Keep the mouth and eyes closed.
- Start the *'hum'* sound with exhalation.

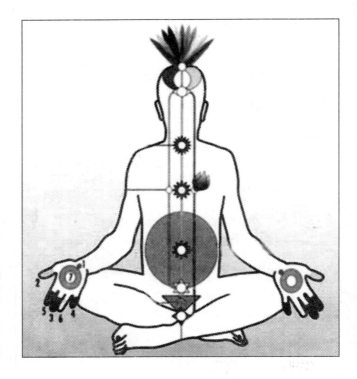

- Feel the relaxation with each *'hum'*.
- When relaxed, bring your palms on your naval.
- Let the open palms face upward under naval.
- Continue with *'hum'*.
- Feel the energy in and around.
- Spread the palms to shower the energy around.
- With hands on naval, say *'hum'* for some time.
- Let the open palms face downwards now.
- Gather the universal energy from around.
- Bring palms on naval and place it in your naval.
- Feel the give-and-take of energy with universe.
- Lie down on your back with eyes closed.
- Feel the oneness with the universe for a while.
- Find yourself ready for the energy work.
- Slowly open the eyes and start the routine.

## CHAKRA MEDITATION

- ❖ Sit in a comfortable position.
- ❖ Close your eyes.
- ❖ Feel your crown and root *charkas*.
- ❖ Allow the divine energies flow thro' them.
- ❖ Feel the energies in them getting balanced.
- ❖ Feel your third eye and sacral *charkas*.
- ❖ Allow the divine energies flow thro' them.
- ❖ Feel the energies in them getting balanced.
- ❖ Feel your throat and solar plexus *charkas*.
- ❖ Allow the divine energies flow thro' them.
- ❖ Feel the energies in them getting balanced.
- ❖ Feel the alignment of all these *charkas*.
- ❖ Feel your heart *charka*.
- ❖ Allow the divine energies flow thro' it.
- ❖ Feel the energies in it getting balanced.
- ❖ Feel your heart in alignment with other *charkas*.
- ❖ Feel the energies of all the *charkas* vibrating.
- ❖ Slowly open your eyes and start the routine.

**34**

## MIRROR EXERCISE

- ❖ Sit in front of a mirror.
- ❖ Look at yourself in mirror.
- ❖ Watch all the thoughts that you get while looking at yourself.
- ❖ Keep watching these thoughts for about ten minutes.
- ❖ If you feel restless after a while, even before ten minutes, in the beginning, get up as soon as you become restless.
- ❖ Later after practising this for a fortnight, know that this restlessness is just escapism. Work to overcome it and be there for ten minutes.

✳ ✳ ✳

35

# JYOTI TRATAK

**TRATAK** is looking at some point with total concentration. As you do that, slowly and steadily your thoughts start getting reflected in the thing you are looking at. This is treated as a good method of introspection and reflection on any important matter.

For doing this, you need to sit in a dark place with least possible wind around. Light a ghee lamp and place it on the level of your eyes about one and a half feet away from you.

Now start looking at the flame as far as possible without blinking the eyes. Keep doing this till your eyes do not get heavy and till you can comfortably look at the flame.

When you feel you cannot look at the flame any more simply lie down at the same place and, if possible, continue lying down. When the eyes get heavy, just close them and lie still for some time.

This exercise increases the eye power, concentration and mind power and has a great potential to relax.

✱ ✱ ✱

# 36

# DEVELOPING YOUR OWN MEDITATION

**AS** you must have got by now, meditation is a tool to give you absolute relaxation, increased concentration and increased productivity, in your regular life. Unless and until you are peaceful, stable and contended in the practical life, you cannot grow in the spiritual path. So, when you want to start on the path of meditation, you may pick up some meditation methods from the listed meditations and follow it or you may design and coin your meditation. This can be a tailor-made meditation for you.

You may follow the following tips for developing your own meditation:

- Check while you want to meditate.
- Separate the reasons you want to escape.
- Work to handle these things practically.
- List out remaining things.
- Check your rituals, check the needs etc.
- Zero down on the most important things.
- Study the aspects of it till you get way.
- Focus on this thing and your breathing.
- Follow on your inner voice.
- Close your eyes when you feel.
- Follow no rule other than your own inner rule.

## COMING OUT OF THE DOING TRAP

**DOINGNESS** is such a strong trap that one really has to work hard to come out of it. Methods, rites, rituals, desire to achieve anything, material or non-material all these things form an integral part of this trap.

Just watch, when you are about to introduce yourself to anyone, what do you think? What do you plan? Are you comfortable just by saying, "hi, I am ...." if the person to whom you are interacting with is not having any clue about your personality? Certainly not! You will try to tell what you do as you introducing yourself. You will say, "hello, I am..... (profession), working in ....company. I like to ....... I have done......... I am planning to do ......." Just watch the whole introduction carefully. Do you see any being anywhere? Do you see anything other than doing? Do you see anything other than getting an identity in the shadow of some action or achievement?

This I call a trap of doing. I know the readers must be thinking by now as to what other way can it be to express your identity? If you just say, "I am ...." what will people know? And after all whatever name and fame you have got till now is just because you have done a few things. Can anyone deny this? Certainly not!

Then, how is this introduction a trap? Let me explain: Trap is not in the introduction. Trap is in the identification. We tell others what we did. They are concerned with the acts that you did and contributed into their lives. These people respect the act, not the person who did the act. But the person who did that act has identified himself with the act and so are the people at large. This is the reason why a person is known by his deeds and adored by his deeds. When people know him or adore him, a person feels happy thinking that he is adored; there he must remember that it is not the person but the deed that is adored. If the same act would have been done by any other person people would have respected and adored that other person. The doer of the act is worshipped just because act is abstract and common man cannot worship anything abstract. He needs something concrete.

The trap is putting you in the position of the act and accepting the worship of the people, or putting yourself in the position of the act that is ridiculed and feel yourself ridiculed.

Then you realize that it is you who are doing. So you are different from the act. If you really want your recognition search it away from what you do or did. If your actions are mistaken as your recognition, the real you will be lost. The doing trap makes you lose yourself like this!

## 38

## IMAGINATION, VISUALIZATION, HALLUCINATION, ILLUSION AND MEDITATION

**MANY** a time, people start their meditation by visualizing something. Then they report that they can see some things or hear some noises etc.

About such visions or sounds that are exclusively experienced by the seeker who is meditating, we have to know that these experiences may be true, but with due regards to the seeker, we cannot forget that these can be illusions or hallucinations and not the real extra sensory perceptions of our conscious mind. Here we are having all the freedom to create any image and imagine it!

If we have a good ability to imagine the visual aspect of the thing or event we mentally create, we can easily see it happening mentally. This is visualization. So, visualizing is just the process of our conscious mind. It has nothing to do with spirituality.

Yet many methods of meditation and spirituality begin with visualization that is purely mental and in no way whatsoever spiritual.

When one starts using this sector of mind called imagination beyond a certain limit, he starts mistaking the created image or imagination as real. This is an illusion.

Illusion is seeing or experiencing something that is not there. We are all aware that when a lie is repeated thousand times, it starts appearing to be the truth. Then, with the same rule, why will the imagination not start appearing as a spiritual experience?

Such a spiritual experience is not actually an experience but an illusion or hallucination. The person having it starts feeling just a hallucination! It is these people who make a big noise about the experiences which do not actually shift their life!

I must share here that the real experiences many a time take time to be recognized. Once, when I was casually meditating and sending healing to some persons, I felt some pushing sensation on my root. It was quite intensely sending the healing and felt that sensation as a disturbance. So, I just told the energies to stop any internal nonsense!

The sensation continued, without my conscious knowledge: I happened to go out of my body and see what it was. It was a stream of golden light. I allowed it to enter my body. The stream of golden light rushed through my root and went straight up to my crown, through all the *chakras*. This was totally unexpected. Suddenly I felt my healing was happening much powerfully. In a while the person to whom I was sending the healing called and reported that he was fine and perfect. I felt happy and started my work. I had forgotten about the golden stream, but the whole day. I found that everything I was doing was happening in the best way. Later after a few days, casually when I shared this experience with a spiritual master, he was taken aback. He said it was the *Kundalini* awakening!

Later, after a few days, I saw a very powerful white light, when I was just lying down peacefully doing nothing. This white light started showering in all my *chakras* and filled my whole body. I felt as if I was merging with the light. It was a wonderful feeling. I did not want to be out of it, but the telephone bell rang and reluctantly I got up and picked up the phone and attended to my patient. Later, after a few days, I realized that it was *"Satori"*, the enlightenment!

These experiences shifted my life, but I had neither visualized anything nor imagined or desired any experiences.

Then, one day, I was practising the unification of *chakras*. Suddenly, I saw a bright ruby red color. I thought I have done some mistake. So I opened my eyes. In fact, the colour was so tempting that I wanted to keep looking at it, but it was so bright that I felt I cannot take it! I closed my eyes and started again. Again the same thing happened. When this happened twice, I thought I was doing some mistake. But, the last time, I saw a white hand along with the ruby red colour! I asked for forgiveness to the master and got up. Later the spiritual master told me that it was blessing of masters I had received! I started using that colour in healing. It was the colour of pure love!

Later from the October of 1995, a weird thing started happening. I used to work as a lecturer in a college then. Daily I would travel by bus from my home to the college. I have a habit of writing while travelling. So, my book and pen is always with me as I travel. These days, suddenly, I would see some figures like some alphabets or script in some unknown language. These would come with some colours tool out of curiosity; I would just copy the figure on some paper available. This was happening on and off. Suddenly on 30th December 1995, while talking about this to another Reiki teacher friend of mine, I saw that all these figures were drawn on the same paper and that they had formed four groups. As I was looking at them in astonishment, as this was not the order in which I had seen them, a name flashed into my mind. The name that I saw was *"Vishitao"*. As I talked about the name that flashed my mind, my friend left on realizing that I had started having some messages again. So I started looking at the figures again. Now the name for each figure started flashing again. This was happening the whole evening. In the night from 12.00 to 4.00 am I was writing as if somebody was dictating. The whole study material for the system called *Vishitao* was written. When I finished with writing, I heard a voice order me that since this is a new year's gift to humanity, I must start teaching it from 1st Jan' 96.

The whole thing was just unbelievable; I called my friends to learn it on 1st Jan. All found the method to be extraordinarily useful. I was convinced that this vision was really a message from the other world.

Then, when I saw Dr. Usui and got the advanced Reiki symbol from him, my skepticism was much less. Yet, I was fully convinced when recently I saw the full size photo of Dr. Usui as the net. Also the power of this symbol was widely tested by my friends and students.

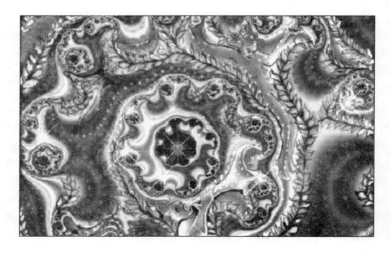

After this, when I received Karyo, it was still a different experience. I had called a get-together meeting of the students as many of my students wanted to meet me for the Guru Purnima. I wished I could give them some energy gift and suddenly I saw the first four layers of Karyo. I shared this with one of my Reiki students who is my father's age. When I described the symbol to him over the phone, he encouraged me to give it to all my Reiki students in the meeting. I was still not clear about the name of the symbol. When I was talking to my Reiki students in the meeting suddenly I found that I told the name "Karyo" during my speech. I knew that masters had given me the name. Later the fifth layer unfolded. At the same time, when the sixth layer was seen, I found that the red energy of it was very strong. I was afraid to receive it; I was again talking to this senior Reiki student of mine who encouraged me to receive it. He said that since the masters feel that I can receive it, they have given it to me. Then the next layers started unfolding till the whole 51-petal lotus of creation called Karyo was fully received. It is now working wonders with my Reiki students!

Now these visions and signals are so casually clear that they come anytime, anywhere! I share them only when it is needed, other times I just follow them.

All this will clearly show that the analytical mind is always analyzing every experience and does not accept it till he is fully convinced that the experience is neither illusion nor hallucination, but the real contact with the other world.

When I heard the words of Dr. Usui that people have made a business of Reiki which he does not like, I had just thought that I was hearing my own thought as a hallucination, but when I read that Dr. Usui was strictly against advertising, I was convinced that I had really heard Usui sensei's words!

Other times, you may see or hear the future events and later they come true. This is really clairvoyance. When I was giving Reiki to Mumbai on 2nd September 1994, heard the words as I saw some focus coming out of the Earth and vanishing. The words said, "You saved Mumbai, but on Anant Chaturdashi's night, there will be a big earthquake in Maharashtra and you won't be able to do anything! I thought I am dreaming and did share it with anyone; actually on the same Anant Chaturdashi night, there was a bad earthquake in Latoor!

So, if you see something about future, do take care to handle the event, but accept it as a message only when you see the evidence of it in reality.

Remember, the visions or messages do not come when you want to receive them, but when masters wish to give them and you are ready to receive them.

Generally, meditation is associated with visions and extrasensory perceptions. But when we start imagining or mentally creating the images, our own doingness starts polluting or suppressing the real visions. So the imagining type of meditations may be used for relaxation, not for **spiritual growth**.

I must also bring to your notice the friend's dream theory here. He says that our mind has a tendency to see our unfulfilled desires fulfilled in our dreams. This is a kind of internal defence to prevent depression and frustrations.

So, whenever you see or hear or dream something that does not really exist, check if it is the thing you wanted but could not get. If yes, know that your vision or experience may be a hallucination by the defence mechanism. So, do not take it as an ESP vision on its face. Such a vision may also be your inner fear manifested. So, when you see a negative event as a vision, check if it is your inner fear because at times our fears too come as hallucinations or dreams. A common vision dream of this type that I used to experience was seeing that I am reaching the exam hall much after the exam paper has started. This used to happen when my exam used to be on. The reason for this used to be the comments by the parents that I am being too lazy and should get ready fast for exam. Later I found that many students have a similar dream or hallucination. If in meditation you see any such thing, check if it is a signal of manifested fear.

Remember, when meditation happens and contact with the other world gets established on its own, whatsoever you see or hear is received casually without any special excitement.

Your mind is stable and grounded after any vision whatsoever!

Let me share one such instance. Nearly a year before Kargil war, I had seen some rocket launchers on a normal road and found myself inside a bunker, as I was in meditation. I did not understand what I was seeing. Suddenly I heard, "Pakistan is going to drop an atom bomb on Mumbai". This was a shocking statement, I still kept my eyes closed and started seeing further. I saw a red fire ball as big as the setting sun right up in the sky. Then I saw it getting surrounded by black smoke. I requested the masters to dissolve it there and then before it would materialize. It did vanish immediately after getting up. I shared this vision with those whom I knew were connected with politics and defence and told them that they must do whatever they can to prevent this event and I will do whatever I can. Nearly a year later, Kargil war happened.

That time it was revealed that Pakistan had taken possession of some bunkers when actually I had seen the bunkers. Then about two years after the war, there were news that Pakistan was all set to drop an atom bomb on India.

I still felt that the word "Mumbai" might be out of my fear, but my logic be possible as Mumbai is the business capital of India. So, if Mumbai is finished, India may lose its major strength!

If in meditation you get any vision of national or global importance, check the vision, share it with your friends and concerned authorities and work on it. You might be able to cause a great contribution to the entire humanity!

Remember, when the masters feel that there is some mishap you can avoid, they give you the vision about it. At other times, something may happen and even if it is happening in front of you, you may not realize it!

This happened with me on the 26th of Jan when there was a major earthquake in Gujarat and Bhuj.

I heard the glasses of my wall unit making noise, I felt the ground trembling, but still it never occurred to me that it's an earthquake.

Nearly half an hour after the tremor stopped, I realized that it was an earthquake! It's evident that the energies did not want my interference! This proves that if you get any vision and signal you, as a healer, are allowed to work on the planned event and change it the way you find it better.

Hence, when you get any vision during your meditation, check that it is not an illusion. Then work on it with your energies to make it better!

## KRIYAS IN MEDITATION

**THE** most common things that the seekers experience are the *kriyas*. Many seekers have a firm faith that no meditation is fruitful without *kriyas*. As you grow in the meditation field, it is said that you start experiencing *kriyas*. Then you know that something is really happening to you and that you have started growing great. Then one day *kriyas* stop happening and you feel that you are going wrong. You yearn for the *kriyas* and they do not happen. At this point, many lose the charm in the meditation and leave the meditation completely. Others may approach their teacher and get the answer to this situation!

Let me explain first of all that actually happens as the *kriyas* happen. When you go into deep level of meditation which

simply means intense concentration, the *Kundalini* energy that is stationed in your root *chakra* in a coiled form starts rising and going towards the crown; just as the mere level in the thermometer starts rising when heat is more. Then when there are obstructions in its path of rising due to non-aligned *chakras* or some energy blocks of thoughts and conditioning, the energy gets a jerk that is felt by the whole body. Sometimes some feel it involuntary due to this jerk. Such a jerk is *kriya*!

Naturally when you have more blocks, you have more *kriyas!* Each time when a *kriya* happens, the energy pushes the block away to create a way. When a smooth way is created and established for the energy, the *kriyas* stop happening. This is the sign of being free from inner blocks! Knowing this fact is vitally necessary in meditation. When *kriyas* stop happening, know that now your real journey has started. Till now the energy was lost in going up. Now it can connect to the other world!

# KNOWING IN MEDITATION

**IN** meditation, when the *kriyas* stop and proper meditation starts happening, a person finds that he can go into trance just with a little bit of will.

Then, with any question in mind, if you concentrate a bit, you find that suddenly the answer to your question flashes into your mind. Logically you may not know why you are thinking in that way, but you just know that is the solution to your problems or that is the way in which you must do the action you want to do.

Yet if somebody else is doing it the other way, you can remain cool and explain that person the right way to go about. There is no hyperactivity or excitement in this case.

This knowledge comes as an inner awareness. The seeker knows about something and this knowledge of the sun is the sky! Such a knowing comes not as a vision or image but just as a thought flashing in mind!

✳ ✳ ✳

**41**

## SATORI AND MEDITATION

**THERE** might be many definitions of *Satori* enlightenment. Here I am describing what I experienced in my own spiritual journey.

First all let me tell that when I started my rigorous meditations, I had nothing special to achieve. I just felt that I should meditate. So I was meditating! After a few days, I started getting a feeling that I am floating and that I am seeing myself in the meditation. I used to meditate not in the sitting position but in sleeping position or *Shavasana*. So, I used to treat these things just as dreams thinking that I am falling off to deep sleep! But once what happened was certainly not a dream. I had invited my friend and her son, but forgot it and went into deep meditation. When she came, my mother called me but I was very deep into meditation and seeing it my friend told my mother that it's ok, I should not be disturbed and that she will come later. When I got up, my mother told me about it and I asked: did she wear a dark blue pure silk with pink print on it! My mother got a shock and asked how I knew this. I simply said I do not know but I know I was watching the whole instance from somewhere at the level of the fan! This was the time I realized that I was actually going out of my body as I was in meditation!

The meditations were going in. One day I suddenly felt that I can offer my self to the existence and let the energies carry on any healing through me! I do not know why I felt quite happy as I mentally said this. A few days later, I started saying in the morning that I was going to have high fever. My friend was at my place when I was saying this. She said that I was saying this just because I did not want to go to my work! I too agreed that this was possible, but by 10.00 am, I really started having fever. By afternoon it was very high as if my body was burning from within. I was sleeping as if I was unconscious. By 4.00 in the afternoon, I felt like having a cold water bath. I just had no energy even to get up, but I had a strong inner drive to take cold water bath. I just called up another healer and told him everything and requested him to keep giving me distance Reiki support to keep me away from fainting as I would take bath. My cousin brother had come to visit us. I had no energy to even talk to him. I took overhead bath with cold water and though it was summer took nearly four blankets and slept. I was almost unconscious, out of my body. This state remained till about 10.30 pm. I heard my cousin calling his home and telling something was seriously wrong with me and that he would not leave my house till I was all right, as no one other than my old mother was at home. He even tried to call me and at the end started checking my pulse and breath to check whether I am alive or not! I could see the concern on his face but was not able to say anything! I just wanted to tell him that I was alright and would get up soon! By 10.30 pm I opened my eyes. Both my cousin and my mother were very relieved! I got up as if there was nothing! I started my work, like cooking etc. I just told my cousin to see the next day's paper. I do not know why I said this. Next day there was news that there was a major fire in the chemical factory in Mumbai that broke at about 10.00 am. The fire fighting started but only by 4.00 pm the fire started coming down and by 10.30 pm it was fully extinguished! The news said that despite a major fire

*Easy Guide to* MEDITATION

that too in the day time, there was not a single casualty! The fire could even have spread in nearby factories but that too did not happen.

I realized that existence had used my body to handle these fire energies! With a genuine heart, I thanked the masters considering me worthy of such a great service! Then, once, I was watching my thoughts. After a while, I closed my eyes. The thoughts had started vanishing.

I suddenly saw a very bright light, brighter than thrice the brightness of the sun! It was coming towards me! It started entering my *chakras* and started filling my whole body! I was with this light for quite some time. At least, I felt so!

Later I realized this was *Satori* enlightenment. That day later on, I was in a totally different world! I am sure if this was just an experience, its effect might have been temporary but this shifted my life in a total way. I was able to be much more composed and cool in most of the situations where a normal person would get too hyper. Also

I would get an indication from within when to get hyper and when not while facing any situation of life or death importance. So, which-ever way I would react in any situation. I would have full control over myself and my expression!

This was the effect of enlightenment! Many people think that this is the ultimate stage in meditation, but let me tell you that this is just the beginning of the spiritual path, where you get the power of stability of mind and connection with the divine to let you go ahead.

If spirituality is like school and college, we must say that wanting to meditate is getting the address of the school. Rising of the *Kundalini* is like getting into the door steps of the school and enlightenment is like getting admission in the school (obviously in nursery or lower K.G.).

So, we cannot know that the real spirituality and spiritual growth begins after enlightenment. Hence, it is not the end point but the real starting point of spirituality.

The *Satori* experienced by all may be different, but at the end all experience self control with constant divine guidance and support and protection. After this enlightenment, whenever one wants he can be in meditation. Then he need not do meditation as he becomes one.

## 42

## DOING AND BEING MEDITATION

**ALL** know that people do meditation. By now the readers must have understood that meditation has to happen. You cannot do it. It is like love when it happens, it is spontaneous intense and natural. When you do it, it is superficial, artificial and unnatural.

To reach the divine and the inner consciousness, you need to go into meditation deeply, spontaneously, intensely and naturally. This cannot happen if you insist on doing it!

It is true that you have to be still and centred to allow meditation happen. But this much is enough!

Nothing beyond this really needed.

In doing this, there is struggle, there is a method, there is desire to reach somewhere. There is a wish to have visions and experiences. There is a fear that we may do mistake, there is an effort to strictly follow the rules, regulations and method of meditation. In all this, the seeker becomes quite rigid, stress-conditioned and goes away from him. But if you are away from self, how can you go near God?

Here I will discuss ways to let meditation happen in the best possible way:

The first requirement for meditation to happen is a totally relaxed mind. This relaxation must happen. If you struggle to relax as many do, the more you struggle to relax the more tense you will be. The next thing that is a must is total focus on your self and whatever is going on there. This is a difficult part because every time you try to face yourself, your mind tends to run away and deviate to some other things. It is rightly said that if one is given a choice to face oneself or face the vast possible death, one may choose death! To this limit a common man is afraid to face himself. The stage of relaxation that needs facing yourself and that too while being relaxed is a really difficult one.

The problem one faces is that before facing oneself one will have to accept himself as he is!

There are so many things about us we hate and want to hide from the world as well as from one's own eyes!

When we start facing our own self, all these things start coming in front of us like a bad dream! We try to run away from it very badly but cannot, so start getting tenser!

Meditation requires you to be relaxed in this situation. Those who find if difficult in fact experience *Kriyas*. These *Kriyas* are a result of the inner resistance to the thoughts, memories stored in various parts of our body.

This means, if you really want meditation to happen, you must first consciously start working on your thoughts, memories and attitudes. See which thing you resist the most and which things you are longing for. Which thoughts you like and which you hate. See the part of yourself that you hate due to some thoughts you have and some memories you have.

When you start working on these things, you can be very restless. You may feel like getting up, going away from the place where you are sitting or thinking of something else.

This is actually the real inner struggle. I am giving some tips to overcome it: First, start openly criticizing you whenever you do not like whatever you have done. This will start tearing off all your false self images and make you confront the real you'd.

Secondly, whenever you can, sit with a pen and paper and start writing your thoughts and struggles and memories and all that you want to express about these things. When you start writing you may even feel some emotional outbursts! Let them come. Do not resist even if you feel like crying bitterly. This will help you release the emotions that are suppressed over a period of time. When you are through destroy all the papers you have written on. Preferably, you should burn the papers as your blocks too get burnt with them.

When you feel like stopping for a while as you write, just sit in a comfortable position or lie down on your back and just start watching your thoughts. Allow your mind to wander freely. Do not try to control it in any way whatsoever. Even if you find that your mind is trying to run away from reality do not mind. Let it run. Its running will not be effective as you have caught it running away.

When you are doing this kind of work on your mind, it is a good idea to have some of your friend who too is working on his or her mind to let meditation happen. Both of you must work as ruthless critiques of each other. This will help you in working on your blocks in the best possible way. Moreover, when your friend is showing your blocks and escapist tendencies there is less chance of you feeling bad. Also you do have a chance to give back even if you feel bad by pointing out the shortcomings and escapist acts of your friend too! This will help both of you to comfort yourself and hit and break your own blocks and escapist tendencies by leaving yourself no space to run away from yourself.

Once you start comforting yourself boldly and have nothing within to run away from, you will feel a typical relaxation from within. It is true that there are many things in life that cause stress and struggle in life. But, this inner stress and struggle is the one that takes away most of our ability being ourself freely. Once this inner struggle vanishes the major amount of stress in you.

Then only the external stress remains but now the factors causing inner depletion and making you powerless are absent. So, now you can have the power to handle all the external situations by using your balanced and logical and detached mind as well as your past experiences and their memories about similar situations. With this, you will be able to handle and defuse the stressful situations very effectively.

When you know that the stressful situations too can be well handled by you, you will still start being relaxed in various situations in life. This will increase the inner relaxation further. The more you start this practice, the more are the chances to let meditation happen on its own!

When the relaxation happens from within the only thing you need to do is just lie down or sit down still with eyes closed or open as you wish, doing nothing.

Then just start watching anything that you feel like watching. As you do this, a point will come when you will feel like closing your eyes and think nothing. You may like to be in this state for some time. Be in this state as long as you feel like opening your eyes; open your eyes and get up while doing this, you may even feel that you are sleeping and not meditating! Never mind. This could be meditation happening and you may not be aware of it, so do not mind.

Can you not say that this is a very simple way to let

*Easy Guide to* MEDITATION 95

meditation happen! Also this is a very much effortless method, where when meditation starts having experiences like *Kundalini* awakening or *Satori* and so on. Then you may not even have to close your eyes or concentrate, but can find yourself in meditation just with a simple thought and desire to meditate. In fact, when this happens, you may even say that you can be in meditation all the time, as you are doing your routine work!

This is actually being meditation! Here you know more about meditation. You do not sit to meditate—you do not follow any method of meditation yourself! Everything you do in meditation or talk comes after getting filtered through the divine consciousness. Then you are taken care by the divine grace in any situation whatsoever! In fact, the final target of all those who want to learn to meditate and learn to relax is the same. They want to be relaxed and have divine guidance and protection throughout all the situations in life. This is the only way to achieve it!

## 43

# OVERCOMING ESCAPISM

**EVERY** meditation is actually expected to take you closer to the divine consciousness. We generally search for it outside. This is the reason why there are so many places of worship where we try to find God or God's guidance or divine help or protection.

In fact, we have to know that the real way to God goes only through your own self and your own mind! When this route is clear, you can be in touch with the divine as and when you wish.

If this is so simple, why do all people not follow this? Yes. This is a valid question. The answer too is simple. No one likes to accept the responsibility of one's own mistakes. We always try to blame others for our own sufferings. If we do not find any human being, we blame the stars, the luck, and the occult forces like ghosts or black magic. If we cannot find anything else to blame, we claim to be very practical, we blame the God!

In fact it will not be wrong in any way whatsoever if I say that man created God in order to put the blame of his deeds on him, as he was very sure that this created entity will never come in front of us and prevent us from blaming him. The stone that is worshipped as God silently keeps taking all worships and rituals and offerings. At the same time it keeps taking all the blames that a believer puts on him directly or silently! This has been happening for many years and will continue for many more years to come!

I know this statement may be offering many people for them. I do not mind even saying that I withdraw this statement if they said that by making this statement I am insulting God. Galileo had rightly stated "neither God, nor the earth nor the sun is going to decide his way after reading this book!"

I know that there is a super consciousness that controls everything! Our senses give us limited knowledge, so we cannot see this power. So, we just imagine and believe! But when we worship God, are we really worshipping this superpower? No, we are just expressing our gratitude to some imagination that does not say anything when we blame it for our sufferings which in fact directly or indirectly are caused by our own deeds!

This is escapism! We find this escapism practically everywhere in every religion, in every spiritual path and in most of the meditation method. The path that takes you out of this escapism is not liked by many and so people criticized it. I know some may even criticize this comment of mine!

We promote and follow escapism as it is convenient. It saves our face. When we say God has all the powers and God can do anything, in fact we are dropping all the powers we are born with.

Why do we want to be powerless and still want to keep saying that we want to be powerful?

The answer is: we do not want to be susceptible to any risk of any kind.

Responsibility and power puts us in a position where we are having all the freedom and we are also open to the blame of all our nations!

When we are meditating, we generally concentrate on something outside us, or other than us. This makes us feel good. Sometimes even great! But is it not because we are just shifting our focus from our own shortcomings to something nice? Just give a thought and you will realize that the answer is yes!

When you feel great while the focus is within and, that too, when you are fully observing yourself, you are even watching and noticing your own shortcomings without guilt or shame but with compassion, you must know that meditation is happening in the real sense.

This is the acid test of real meditation without escapism!

But the problem is that first of all people do not realize that through meditation they are trying to escape the real life problems and when somebody tells them so, they do not agree. Then these people start getting into further problems. But they console themselves by saying that as they are spiritually growing, God is testing them by giving them greater problems.

This is a greater sugarcoated escapism that is heard, taught, liked almost everywhere in the spiritual circles!

We always hear people saying that when you go further in the spiritual path, you have to face more hardships. When you meditate more, you are given some fearful experiences that can dissuade you from continuing meditations. There are many mythological stories of this type that we have heard. We certainly, trust all that we hear since our childhood. But how many of us actually try to go to the rest of the truth behind these stories? If you see these difficulties and frightful experiences as the blocks you have created to avoid confronting yourself, then you are absolutely right. These difficulties do come when you struggle and try to run away from facing yourself.

There is yet another way in which one faces difficulties. Here, a person is desperately trying to meditate and follow spiritual practice in order to run away from oneself or from some difficult situations in his life.

Then the problem worsens as it is not handled in time. This worsened problem comes in front of the person and catches him in a tricky situation from which he almost has no escape. Then when he has to handle it or succumb to the problem, he consoles himself by saying that God is testing him.

Can you not see a clear escapism in such cases?

Meditation is not an escape from your problems! Meditation is not going to get you any solution to come out of the problem! Just because you meditate, your problem is not going to vanish on its own!

Remember problem is a problem as long as you call it a problem and don't see and notice solution hidden within it.

Once you notice and know it, it remains any other situation to handle.

Worshipping God, doing meditation, saying *Mantras* etc. have their own advantages, but they certainly cannot be used to escape from problem.

In fact using God to escape is the greatest insult to God and humanity has been doing it for years together.

It is time that there are some situations that we cannot control, but we can still handle their effect on us! Also there are many situations that we do have a power to control and handle. But for that we have to take the responsibility. This means if there is a mistake, we have to accept it and know that we have caused the mistake. This would hurt our ego, but we would have to take it! Our ego is one thing we protest at all the times by paying any cost. So, the suffering is the cost we pay to protest our ego in a number of situations. The trap of escapism lies exactly at this place. We say we want to escape the problem, but in fact when we try to approach spirituality or try to meditate, most of the times, we are trying to escape the hurt to our ego due to the fact that we are not accepting responsibility.

If you wish that meditation should happen to you, you need to know how to handle this type of escapism. Remember, of this, you will have to be on your guard all the time.

Even if you know the theory that you must face yourself to bring it into practice is not so easy. This is one of the things that are easy said and preached than done! Saying that you practise this, and not practising in reality causes greater stress and struggle.

Believe in the super power God is needed, but not before understanding him. Surrender to God is needed. When you do surrender, it is not important, to whom do you surrender to. It is just important that you surrender. You may follow any religion, worship any God, use any prayer, but really the important thing is that you surrender. The absolute surrender lets you forget yourself, and then the all-powerful reflection of the super power remains. Then the *Satori* enlightenment comes. Escapists never experience it. They keep struggling, talking about enlightened masters, keep worshipping them and following them.

They also keep talking about the enlightenment. But what they talk is many times a theory that they have hardly experienced. Those who are struggling to escape hear these stories or read them. Sometimes these stories are given a perfect religious touch. Such stories make the escapists feel better, but in reality, where do they go? The answer is nowhere! When you try to escape your own self, nowhere is the only place where you can go.

This is a bit about the escapism that we find in meditation. In fact there are many more things to say, but I think after seeing, knowing and understanding it, the readers would certainly want and know how to keep away from it and its traps.

# 44

## AWARENESS, ENLIGHTENMENT AND BEYOND

**THE** final point of meditation is supposed to be liberation.

The journey towards it is supposed to begin with self-realization.

Let us start seeing the first step into this journey. Of course the first step that you take is the act of knowing and practising meditation. Then, if you are following the tips that you have read till now, you may experience something called awareness of a witness.

A witness is the one who is very much leading a normal life, but is still not attached to any experience or memory in the sense, he has the power to let go of everything and so nothing can hook him. He knows to take life as it comes. He is acting while doing his work but he knows who to keep away from forced reacting, without inner awareness. This is just not possible.

When you keep meditating with this awareness, a point comes when you find that you are connected to the divine consciousness. Then there comes a point when you experience *Satori* or enlightenment. This makes you be aware of your oneness with the divine.

These stages are already discussed earlier. Now we need to see what happens beyond this. I have already said that

*Satori* is the beginning of the path to total liberation and oneness with the divine.

All this can be called as the path beyond enlightenment.

Enlightenment helps you realize your real nature and the smallness of everything around that you feel and experience. It lets you know that when a moment is gone, it is gone. Then you know that there is no sense in wasting your time over the lost moments. It will be a better idea to create better moments for ourselves by facing and handling life with realistic attitude.

As you start doing this, you notice a number of things that you had left half way, not because you did not know either how to complete them or you were not very clear about your real inner wishes, when you had started to do them. Some of these things are still open to be completed. You can complete them if you so wish. Others have left their effect that you might have already handled.

It is a good idea to start completing things as you proceed in meditation. This will add great peace to your mind.

Initially before you have experienced *Satori*, you may find this very wrong too! You may say something was not completed because it was not to be completed—so what! No problem. But the question was never whether you must complete every action or thing or relationship you started or not. The question was always: whether you are complete about all your actions. If you have any sour or incomplete feelings, complete them.

When you are complete from within, now start looking for what you have, what you do not have, what you want, what you do not what, what you think you can get and what you think you cannot get and so on, and your views and attitudes to all these thoughts, and start completing all the incompletion left in all these thoughts.

Just like this inner completion, enlightenment also starts getting you the material completion. When you are in total surrender to the divine you will find that you are totally taken care of.

Total surrender is accepting all the things that happen as they do and having knowledge (not FAITH) that come what may, you will be taken care of. A person in total surrender does not have to think of his own future. Generally the attitude of such a person is, "If I try to plan my future, I am proving that I do not trust the grave of the divine!"

Remember, total surrender comes out of total non-attachment. Non-attachment does not mean lack of interest in life. It only means lack of expectations of things you have not worked for. When you sincerely work for anything, grace automatically shows you the right direction.

I must also state here that the surrender follows the all or none law that means either you are in total 100% surrender or you are not in surrender at all. Total surrender is not just necessary but mandatory for getting self-realization of any type whatsoever.

But again this surrender is grossly misinterpreted and a person is led to escapism through it too.

So, before surrender you need to know what it actually means. The seeker must know that, to whom he surrenders is not important. The fact that he surrenders is important. This is surrender to the divine self that is actually reflected into your own self. So, in effect, your surrender is to your own inner self in order to surrender to the highest consciousness that is commonly known as God.

It is not necessary to follow any rules, rituals, beliefs, cults or *Gurus* in order to surrender. In fact, when you surrender to anything lower than the highest consciousness that is known as *Nirguna Nirakara* God, you are in fact insulting it. Yet, like the so-called lower Gods and *Gurus*, this super conscious God never gets angry with you. It never gives you any curse or punishment for submitting to a lower God or for being a total non-believer too. So it is never necessary to give offerings and please him. The system of offerings again was created by some intelligent people who knew that they can take advantage of the ignorance and fear of the masses to run their livelihood. So they created the fear of the anger of Gods in the minds of the masses and started making them give offerings which in fact would go to the spiritual *Guru* or the person who is the head of the temple. This way, by doing nothing else, these people could run their livelihood quite luxuriously.

Such an offering is never surrender. It is madness. Such surrender will drain you materially instead of giving you material completeness.

Inner peace, completed things around, completed relationships, full material grounding and prosperity, all these are actually the signs of being in a right path in meditation.

Beyond enlightenment, there are a few hard patches, but they appear only because you have not yet learned true surrender. When true surrender happens, these hard patches dissolve. Then you find that even when the situation that used to make you hyper earlier appears, you are peaceful from within. This time you find that the situation gets handled very easily. Such events give you the realization that surrenders works. But then there are times when you are given difficult situations to face and you do not do anything though you had earlier felt like doing something. You just say that grace will handle it. Such times, you find that nothing works and you have to handle it yourself. Such times you learn a lesson that when you face a difficult situation, you need to follow the signal that grace gives you through your own mind.

As you move on with this journey of surrender, a time comes when you need to grow. Till now you were just being a child. Now you need to be a responsible adult. You need to take some major decisions, at times even of global importance and do the necessary energy work at the necessary level.

You get to know about some event in advance and you do have the power to change or cancel it in favour of humanity or planet earth.

This is reaching adulthood beyond enlightenment. Here you get the powers like creating the events on a certain way just by your thought, seeing and practising future, knowing all the details about a person, not by talking to him for a while, having an insight of a problem on facing it or on hearing about it and so on.

These things may be called clairvoyance, clair audience and *waachaa siddhi* by some. These are ways to develop clairvoyance partially even before this, where you can see the auras of a person and heal it, but the clairvoyance after enlightenment at this stage is much more advanced. Here you can see things far away or from past or future, effortlessly even without having to close your eyes. This is because the vision of your mind is fully active, aware, and powerful.

When you get all these powers, you naturally get the responsibility to handle them in a right way for the benefit of the humanity.

A special and peculiar thing of a master who has reached this adulthood after enlightenment is that he tries to be as transparent and invisible as possible. He keeps leading an absolutely normal life, remains humble as well as practical, does not show off his powers and keeps working silently.

He knows that it is useless to tell those who are in deep sleep that he is awake and there is no need to tell this to those who are already awake. So he is just silent. The test to find such a master is to notice what happens to you when you are in his presence or in his contact. When you find that by just being in touch with somebody who is successful and down-to-earth, things in your life have started falling in right place on their own, you will know that you have met a master who is at this level. Do not talk anything about spirituality, just follow this and see the difference.

As you go on being meditation and advancing further, your power goes on increasing. Then you may even find that, at times, just your thought can cause major positive shifts in many areas. At this stage, a person may do the practical work for himself, but may silently work not just on smaller canvas like his family or so, but works on a bigger canvas like nation or continent or globe.

Such masters are so transparent that a common man may not even know that the person to whom he is interacting is a master of this level. The total absence of pride and total humility along with total let-go with the oneness of the existence make him like this.

This is the state when a person is totally contented and peaceful. He may do his routine, have targets and meet them too, but he may still not long for anything. He would be happy with whatever he has and he has all that he needs, without any struggle.

He looks at all with compassion and has no anger or negative feeling for anyone. He never worries and is always respectful to all.

The company of such a person is pleasant to all. He never runs away from the crowd though at times the people may not give him his own space to be. Still he never allows anyone to treat him as a *Guru* or messenger of God or anything important like this. He feels that this status may create false inflated ego in him, and at the same time he also wants the people to know and acknowledge the real divine not as he describes it, but as they find it themselves.

I am sure there must be many stages of development after this, but I have no desire to write about anything that I have not experienced directly or indirectly. Reading books, compiling the information and writing is done by many, but I do not know how much of that is supported by personal experience. Hence I claim that each and every word I have written here is supported by personal experience.

## BEING MEDITATION IN DAILY LIFE

**WHEN** you know where you can reach by being in meditation regularly, you must also be willing to know how you can be the meditation for all the twenty-four hours of the day as you are following your routine work and leading a normal life in all the worldly sense.

Here I am giving some golden rules for the same:

- Work on your mind daily.
- If you dislike a thing, express it.
- See why you disliked that thing.
- Try to find out an advantage in everything that happens.
- Allow space and freedom to others around you.
- Be assertive about your space and freedom too.
- Handle conflict as soon as it appears and is noticed.
- Drop every struggle as soon as you notice it.
- The moment you find hooked on to a thought, leave that thought.
- Watch everything that you do, feel or think.
- Have discipline not conditioning.

- ❖ Follow the mind, not the ego.
- ❖ Care for others but don't be influenced or biased.
- ❖ Forgive yourself if you want others to forgive you.
- ❖ Love yourself if you want others to love you.
- ❖ The moment you see a problem, detach yourself.
- ❖ Look at your problem as somebody else's problem.
- ❖ Remember problem is a problem as long as you say so.
- ❖ Initially, whenever you are free sit still.
- ❖ The moment you get a chance, start watching your thoughts.
- ❖ When I say these rules will help you become meditation in your daily life, I only mean that you must remember these things in your daily life. You need not bind yourself with these rules, but you may let them create an inner chemical change in yourself so that the struggling, escaping, guilty, powerless, self-denying you vanishes and shifts itself into a powerful, guilt-free peaceful you that emerges!

Also remember a few more things:

- ❖ Don't have a habit of a habit.
- ❖ Don't let any rule bind you ever.
- ❖ Be disciplined out of your free choice.
- ❖ Choose your own ways to follow.
- ❖ Drop all conditioning and rigidity.

Again, these too are no rules. I admit that I followed all these and I am where I am now, in spite of many things that could have devastated my life. All those things in fact contributed to my inner growth and made me internally stronger and cooler.

So even if you are having any problems, you are welcome to the path of meditation, not for successfully escaping the problem, but for successfully handling it. Meditations will give you peace of mind and show you the right way of handling the situation in your life.

The sign of being meditation is that your mind remains still and becomes quieter when you do not know what to do. Normally a person becomes disturbed and upset in such situations, but a master who is now meditation personified knows that this is the situation where his mind has to be totally still. Only then he will be able to see the solution hidden in the problem and receive the divine signals regarding that situation. This master never calls any situation a problem. For him the difference is just that he already knows how to handle some situations whereas he yet has to know how to handle the others.

So, practise all the tips given here and enjoy being meditation in your daily life. Welcome to the world of awareness!

## 46

## ROLE OF GURU IN MEDITATION

**GURU** is teacher. He has already reached the place where you aspire to reach. But he is not selfish to enjoy that position alone. He is ready to help others to grow to that position. He not only teaches a disciple to meditate, but also helps him know where he has reached in his journey, by interpreting the different kinds of experience he gets.

The seeker of the path of meditation needs a right kind of guidance, but unless the *Guru* himself has been in meditation in the right way he cannot help the seeker develop in the right way in meditation.

In the present time, when everything is commercialized, there is no wonder if even the *Gurus* get commercialized! We certainly find many *Gurus* to teach meditation online, who ask you to send a few dollars for the training sessions or CDs of meditation.

It is perfectly all right to have such online *Gurus* provided they know their work well. This means, a seeker must have some acid to find out whether the *Guru* met online is right or not.

Even when you meet a *Guru* in person, whether in city or mountain, you have to test the person with the acid test before taking him as a *Guru* and offering all your spiritual future in his hands.

First test of a right *Guru* is that he is thoroughly practical. The second test is that he does not get stuck into the theories and jargons of words and ideas. The third test is that he does not mind facing and accepting and handling all his faults, shortcomings and criticisms. The fourth is that he is perfect in knowledge and is ready to answer all possible questions. The fifth and the last test is that a right *Guru* is never stuck with any method of seeking spirituality or being in meditation. He is well aware of the methodless method of being in real meditation.

If your *Guru* passes all these tests, know that he is the right one. He might or might not appear as a spiritual person; he might or might not appear to be professional. Yet he will be the one who will have the power to guide you.

## 47

## ROLE OF SILENCE IN MEDITATION

**SILENCE** is absence of words and sounds that appear internally or externally. While talking about silence, we generally think of silence outside around us. But in meditation, the silence that is more important is the silence within. This is not to be forced. It has to be achieved by giving total freedom to the mind.

The common notion is that we must control the mind and should not allow it to wonder, so that it will be silent.

Some people think that the external silence leads to the internal silence. So, they go to the forests or mountains to meditate. In India, Himalaya is the best known place for meditation.

This is a good idea, but we forget that even if you cut the external noise, at such places, you very much carry the noise from within. It is this noise that does not allow meditation to happen.

When we say that meditation happens in silence, the silence that we talk about here is internal and not external. External silence is a bonus!

To achieve the inner silence that is vitally important for meditation, we need to first check all the inner noises and work on them. When the inner noises are strong, we go on

*Easy Guide to* MEDITATION

talking within and go on suppressing this talk to get the silence. All this leads to a lot of restlessness within.

To get the inner silence, suppression is of no use. The best way to get inner silence is to let the mind go wherever it goes, let it think anything it wants, not to stop the mind starts doing all this, watch the actions of the mind, watch every emotion the mind feels, watch all the anxiety mind feels over any issue, watch the pain mind goes through as it thinks about some issue and so on.

When we are doing this, mind feels free to experience anything it wants. As a result, it is no more restless. There is a point when it stops wandering and stays at rest. This is the time when we get the inner silence. Then meditation happens.

As we meditate, before every meditation session, this work on the mind is advisable.

## 48

## ROLE OF SECLUSION IN MEDITATION

**SECLUSION** is staying away from others. Again this is both internal and external. Externally when we are physically isolated we are secluded. But unless and until there is internal seclusion, this is of no use.

When we are mentally with ourselves, we are internally secluded. When this is the situation, there are no distractions due to the inputs by the thoughts, attitudes or comments of others, either in physical reality or on the mental plane.

When we are with others, our thinking automatically and constantly gets affected by the things that we see, hear or experience. This means every time when we try to reactivate inner silence, there is a noise to break that silence. Seclusion avoids this.

But as I say inner seclusion is more important or at least as much important as the outer seclusion. Now let us see what comes in the way of this inner seclusion.

Many times we find ourselves constantly thinking about some person we like or we hate or one who has hurt us and so on. This means mentally we are with the person about whom we are thinking. Then we keep thinking of the reactions and responses of that person from time to time and react to it mentally.

This means even if we are alone, we are not secluded. We may be lonely but not alone. This situation cannot be called seclusion though physically it is so.

In this situation, our thoughts about the persons we are thinking of are breaking the silence and causing distraction.

On the other hand, it so happens at times that we are in a crowd, but we are neither paying attention onto the crowd, nor reacting to anything happening in the crowd. This means the physical presence of people around is not in a position to break the inner silence.

In this situation, we ARE secluded even if physically we are not. Be aware of one thing here: even if we are with many people physically, we are with more in reality as there s no exchange of stimuli and responses as far as we are concerned. Even such seclusion is acceptable for meditation, but only those who are used to be the meditation can meditate in such seclusion.

Others and especially the beginners in the path of meditation cannot use such seclusion for meditation. They need total silence outside and total absence of people around before they start on the path of meditation. If they are not secluded, they cannot concentrate. This actually means, if they are not secluded and left in silence, they cannot work on their mind in any way whatsoever.

So, seclusion is very important in meditation and the external seclusion is needed for those who are new to meditation and are still DOING meditation.

May be this is the reason why people go to forests and mountains when they wish to meditate a lot and reach the spiritual growth.

## 49

# ROLE OF SURROUNDINGS IN MEDITATION

**SURROUNDINGS** are the things, objects and natural environments around you. All these things carry some or the other energies and vibrations. They are good or bad, positive or negative, silent or noisy, peaceful or disturbed.

These surroundings have an impact on our mind. So, they are given lot of value in meditation. The silent, pleasant, peaceful and positive surroundings have a power to make the mind still and peaceful, such a mind can get into meditation quite easily.

When we are in the midst of nature, the balance and harmony is automatically created within. All our imbalances are healed and balance is restored.

This happens just by being with the nature. The natural surroundings have this power.

Of course, the nature is not always positive and pleasant. At times it also becomes highly volatile. This happens especially on the onset of a natural calamity. Then the sensitive minds get upset just by being in the nature.

Many times, people get upset for no reason. They experience some inner fear and yet do not know what is wrong with them.

After some time, the violence of the nature gets evident and they know that it was this that was creating anxiety within them.

It is this effect of nature on us that makes animals behave in a certain way before some natural event or calamity. The rats start running out of their holes before earthquake, the birds fly to a shelter before it starts raining, and fishes vanish from the area of sea that is likely to be struck by sea-storm. All such examples will show you the nature of impact the surroundings have on us if we are sensitive.

For meditation, the good nature plays an important role. It helps us be in the inner silence and puts us in conversation with our inner self after which we can naturally be in meditation.

## 50

## ROLE OF CHANTING IN MEDITATION

**CHANTING** is saying something again and again. It is called *Japa* in Sanskrit. Generally people use some *Mantras* i.e. some sacred words for chanting as they meditate.

Different people use different *mantras* as they meditate. It is said that the vibrations of these *Mantras* help the meditation happen well. I do not deny this fact. But the basic use of chanting is to keep the monkey called mind busy so that it does not keep wandering as we are busy in trying to get in touch with ourselves or with God or anything we are meditating on.

Generally when we are still, our mind keeps wandering, we learn that for meditation there has to be silence within. To achieve this silence, we struggle to catch hold of the mind and stop it from wandering. But this force is just like the force used to make a jumping and extraactive infant keep quiet. The moment we shout on the child, he may reduce his jumping around, but will definitely start screaming and crying loudly. This screaming is worse than its jumping because it gets violent.

Then the wise people give some toy or toffee to the infant so that he forgets jumping or screaming and gets busy with the toy or the toffee.

The chanting does the work of a toy as far as the infant monkey called mind is concerned. The mind that starts jumping as soon as it gets a chance forgets jumping on getting the toy of chanting. It gets busy with chanting.

The chanting is mainly of three kinds: first is loud chanting, second is soft chanting where you are saying the *mantra* but not so loudly that all can hear it while the third is mental chanting where you do not use your tongue at all.

*Yoga* treats the third type of chanting as the best. It is believed some sound vibrations and these vibrations produce some results in our system.

This is a fact. I have seen the results the *mantras* produce. I know a *mantra* that is used for protection and for healing the inner disturbance. This *mantra* is *"Hoom Phat Swaha"*. When this *mantra* is recited 501 times, we can find an electric white protection shield created around a person who is chanting it as well as around a person for whom it is being chanted. This shield can be seen by the persons who are clairvoyant and can see the aura. Others can even sense this shield by touching it. In fact, if you try to approach the shield with a negative intention for the protected person, you may even feel a shock of repulsion!

So, this is the power of *Mantra* chanting. The chanting as we have already seen is known as *Japa*. When due to constant chanting, the *Japa* becomes an automatically reflex action as breathing, it is known as *Ajapajapa*. That is chanting without chanting.

This too is treated as a very important element of meditation. When the chanting starts happening, even the meditation can start happening subsequently.

# 51

## ROLE OF POSTURE IN MEDITATION

**POSTURE** is the position in which we sit or lie down. It is believed that certain postures like lotus posture are excellent for good meditation.

Yet, many find it difficult to sit in that posture for a very long time: they start getting restless and want to be out of that posture as fast as possible.

Still they keep insisting that they must be in the same posture just because many people say that this is the right posture for meditation.

I must say here that though it is ideal to have spine straight, it is also a vitally important requirement of meditation. So even if you meditate in normal sitting posture with spine straight with support or in *Shavasana* where you lie straight on your back, it is perfectly fine.

The posture of a person is supposed to be complementary to the other factors necessary to focus the mind on the thing we are meditating on. At the same time we must know that real meditation can happen only after a person reaches the state of deep relaxation. So, the posture that we take while in meditation must always help us remain in the relaxed state.

All this is certainly necessary in the beginning. Later on,

when you get used to be in meditation in any posture whatsoever, then even while travelling in a train that is extremely crowded, where you are barely standing on one leg, holding your bag in one hand and hanging on to some support with the other as you barely get fresh air to breathe you may not be able to stand comfortably, but you can definitely meditate comfortably. Have you ever imagined that even such a horrible situation and posture can be taken to be good enough for meditation, once it starts happening on its own!

Anyway, my personal advice is: it is good to sit in the lotus posture with tip of the tongue touching upper palate as you begin meditation. But see to it that you sit on a bed like this and any time during meditation when you feel uncomfortable being in this posture, just lie down on your back in *Shavasana* and continue with the meditation as long as you wish to be, and see the effect!

## 52

## ROLE OF PLACE IN MEDITATION

**PLACE** is the actual place or premises where you meditate. We all know that every place carries some vibrations. These are positive, negative or neutral. Of these, the positive vibrations are best for meditation and the neutral ones are all right. But the negative vibrations cause upsets and prevent the happening of meditation.

Also, the meditation state being the state of deep relaxation, one is very susceptible to any intrusion. So, if one enters this state in the presence of negative energies, one is likely to face a psychic attack as one is in meditation.

I am not trying to scare or put off those who want to meditate. I am just stating a fact. At the same time I would be showing the way to handle such situation and its effects.

First of all, when you think of sitting for meditation, you need to check the place. This can be done by simply seeing your inner voice and finding out whether you are internally happy or unhappy by being in that place. If you feel good and happy within, then know that it is the right place for meditation. You can safely meditate there. Then start with meditation.

If you do not feel internally happy and peaceful check what you feel. If this feeling is neutral, then too it is all right to meditate there. But if you are feeling restless and upset from within, then know that that place is not the right place for meditation. Then never ever start meditating just for the sake of it. The meditation will not happen in that place.

The vibrations of the place are responsible for the kind of thoughts you get as you relax. If the vibrations are good and positive, you will get positive and constructive thoughts. If the vibrations are bad and negative, you will get negative and destructive thoughts.

When the thoughts gain power, the events we have thought of materialize. This means, if we think of constrictive things as we meditate, they come true in future. Similarly, if we think of destructive things as we meditate the things we think of end up in damaging us to great extent. This happens both in case of auto-generated as well as consciously generated thoughts. So, as long as we are not strong enough and as long as the place has the power to generate thoughts in us, we need to be careful of the place when we meditate.

## 53

## ROLE OF KNOWLEDGE IN MEDITATION

**KNOWLEDGE** is awareness of facts. These facts come to us either by way of learning, or reading or seeing or experiencing. The level of knowledge received by each way is different. The last one produces the deepest impact on a person.

When we store some information as knowledge, it produces a deep conditioning within us. Then our thinking and responses are governed by our knowledge and so are our wishes and expectations.

When we meditate many times this knowledge becomes a hindrance in it. When we start looking within and start noticing our experiences about many things, we start interpreting them logically and at times miss out in the real experience. This means, due to our pre-notion about something due to our so-called knowledge, we expect some kind of experience and feel that any nearby alike experience is the one that we have expected. This is how a number of times the illusions are taken as real things because we feel that we experience them. We also tend to be quite firm on our belief that our experience was not an illusion and say that we know!

For a right kind of meditation, therefore, just as knowledge is good at a number of times even unlearning in necessary.

Yet knowledge is given a great value not only in meditation but in all fields of life. People read, they learn, they share from others and claim to know. Very few actually care to experience and know. If the foundation of knowledge is not actual practical experience that has come out of neutral attitude and open mind, then all the knowledge is just shallow and cannot take us anywhere. Yet those who have this kind of knowledge are too stubborn about it and are fanatic about their knowledge and the rituals and methods given in that knowledge.

So remember if you want to be in real meditation, first, gain as much knowledge as you can about meditation, and study all the things you learn well. Then drop all those things and have an open mind. Just start watching all your thoughts, attitudes, likes and dislikes, struggles and so on with no bias whatsoever. This will let you be in real meditation.

# APPENDIX

To meditate is to concentrate fully on something and to assimilate it fully with total awareness.

✳✳✳

When we are doing anything, we are never one with the thing we are doing.

✳✳✳

When you are totally relaxed and are in total surrender to anything that you are doing, meditation is happening to you.

✳✳✳

Those who know how to allow meditation to happen know how to remain relaxed in all situations and how to overcome the anxiety even if it appears in some situation.

✳✳✳

*Yoga* means a path of a seeker. We have eight stages of it, namely, *yama, niyama, pranayama, aasana, pratyahar, dhyan, dharana* and *samadhi*.

✻✻✻

Meditation is a tool to give you absolute relaxation, increased concentration and increased productivity, in your regular life.

✻✻✻

If your actions are mistaken as your recognition, the real you will be lost. The doing trap makes you lose yourself like this!

✻✻✻

When contact with the other world gets established, whatsoever you see or hear is received casually. Your mind is stable and grounded after any vision whatsoever!

✻✻✻

When you have more blocks, you have more *kriyas*! Each time when a *kriya* happens, the energy pushes the block away to create a way.

❋❋❋

The knowledge through meditation comes as an inner awareness just as a thought flashing in mind!

❋❋❋

When we feel great while the focus is within, you must know that meditation is happening in the real sense. This is the acid test of real meditation without escapism!

❋❋❋

Meditation is not an escape from your problems!

❋❋❋

When you try to escape your own self, nowhere is the only place where you can go.

❋❋❋

A witness is the one who is leading a normal life, but is not attached to any experience or memory. Nothing can hook him. He knows to take the life as it comes.

✳✳✳

Total surrender is accepting all the things that happen as they do and having knowledge (not faith) that come what may, you will be taken care of.

✳✳✳

The total surrender comes out of total non-attachment.

✳✳✳

Non-attachment does not mean lack of interest in life. It only means lack of expectations of things you have not worked for.

✳✳✳

Inner peace, completed things around, completed relationships, full material grounding and prosperity; all these are actually the signs of being in a right path in meditation.

✳✳✳

The total absence of pride and total humility along with total let go with the oneness of the existence are the tests of a real transparent master.

✸✸✸

The sign of being meditation is that your mind remains still and becomes quieter when you do not know what to do.

✸ ✸ ✸

## QUOTES TO SEE DAILY

God created us with love and respect.
Let us keep the same respect for god!
Don't treat him as a tool to put blame on!

✳ ✳ ✳

Meditation is putting yourself in touch
with your own real inner self!

✳ ✳ ✳

Live the love for your self and you will
express the love for god!

✳ ✳ ✳

Run away from yourself and the doors of
self-made hell are opening for you!

✳ ✳ ✳

# HEALTHS Books

**David Servan Schreiber (Guerir)**
- The Instinct to Heal — 195.00
  (Curing stress, anxiety and depression without drugs and without talk therapy)

**M. Subramaniam**
- Unveiling the Secrets of Reiki — 195.00
- Brilliant Light — 195.00
  (Reiki Grand Master Manual)
- At the Feet of the Master (Manal Reiki) — 195.00

**Sukhdeepak Malvai**
- Natural Healing with Reiki — 100.00

**Pt. Rajnikant Upadhayay**
- Reiki (For Healthy, Happy & Comfortable Life) — 95.00
- Mudra Vigyan (For Health & Happiness) — 60.00

**Sankalpo**
- Neo Reiki — 150.00

**Dr. Shiv Kumar**
- Aroma Therapy — 95.00
- Causes, Cure & Prevention of Nervous Diseases — 75.00
- Diseases of Digestive System — 75.00
- Asthma-Allergies (Causes & Cure) — 75.00
- Eye-Care (Including Better Eye Sight) Without Glasses — 75.00
- Stress (How to Relieve from Stress A Psychlogical Study) — 75.00

**Dr. Satish Goel**
- Causes & Cure of Blood Pressure — 75.00
- Causes & Cure of Diabetes — 60.00
- Causes & Cure of Heart Ailments — 75.00
- Pregnancy & Child Care — 95.00
- Ladie's Slimming Course — 95.00
- Acupuncture Guide — 50.00
- Acupressure Guide — 50.00
- Acupuncture & Acupressure Guide — 95.00
- Walking for Better Health — 95.00
- Nature Cure for Health & Happiness — 95.00
- A Beacon of Hope for the Childless Couples — 60.00
- Sex for All — 75.00

**Dr. Kanta Gupta**
- Be Your Own Doctor — 60.00
  (a Book about Herbs & Their Use)

**Dr. B.R. Kishore**
- Vatsyana Kamasutra — 95.00
- The Manual of Sex & Tantra — 95.00

**Dr. M.K. Gupta**
- Causes, Cure & Prevention of High Blood Cholesterol — 60.00

**Acharya Bhagwan Dev**
- Yoga for Better Health — 95.00
- Pranayam, Kundalini aur Hathyoga — 60.00

**Dr. S.K. Sharma**
- Add Inches — 60.00
- Shed Weight Add Life — 60.00
- Alternate Therapies — 95.00
- Miracles of Urine Therapy — 60.00
- Meditation & Dhyan Yoga (for Spiritual Discipline) — 95.00

- A Complete Guide to Homeopathic Remedies — 120.00
- A Complete Guide to Biochemic Remedies — 60.00
- Common Diseases of Urinary System — 95.00
- Allopathic Guide for Common Disorders — 125.00
- E.N.T. & Dental Guide (in Press) — 95.00
- Wonders of Magnetotherapy — 95.00
- Family Homeopathic Guide — 95.00
- Health in Your Hands — 95.00
- Food for Good Health — 95.00
- Juice Therapy — 75.00
- Tips on Sex — 75.00

**Dr. Renu Gupta**
- Hair Care (Prevention of Dandruff & Baldness) — 75.00
- Skin Care — 75.00
- Complete Beautician Course (Start a Beauty Parlour at Home) — 95.00
- Common Diseases of Women — 95.00

**Dr. Rajiv Sharma**
- First Aid (in Press) — 95.00
- Causes, Cure and Prevention of Children's Diseases — 75.00

**Dr. R.N. Gupta**
- Joys of Parenthood — 40.00

**M. Kumaria**
- How to Keep Fit — 20.00

**Dr. Pushpa Khurana**
- Be Young and Healthy for 100 Years — 60.00
- The Awesome Challenge of AIDS — 40.00

**Acharya Satyanand**
- Surya Chikitsa — 95.00

**Dr. Nishtha**
- Diseases of Respiratory Tract (Nose, Throat, Chest & Lungs) — 95.00
- Backache (Spondylitis, Cervical Arthritis, Rheumatism) — 95.00
- Ladies Health Guide (With Make-up Guide) — 95.00

**L.R. Chowdhary**
- Rajuvenate with Kundalini Mantra Yoga — 95.00

**Manoj Kumar**
- Diamond Body Building Course — 95.00

**Koulacharya Jagdish Sharma**
- Body Language — 125.00

**G.C. Goyal**
- Vitamins for Natural Healing — 95.00

**Dr. Vishnu Jain**
- Heart to Heart (with Heart Specialist) — 95.00

**Asha Pran**
- Beauty Guide (With Make-up Guide) — 75.00

**Acharya Vipul Rao**
- Ayurvedic Treatment for Common Diseases — 95.00
- Herbal Treatment for Common Diseases — 95.00

**Dr. Sajiv Adlakha**
- Stuttering & Your Child (Question-Answer) — 60.00

---

Books can be requisitioned by V.P.P. Postage charges will be Rs. 20/- per book.
For orders of three books the postage will be free.

## ◉ DIAMOND POCKET BOOKS

X-30, Okhla Industrial Area, Phase-II, New Delhi-110020, Phone : 011-51611861, Fax : 011-51611766
E-mail : sales@diamondpublication.com, Website : www.fusionbooks.com

# Some books which you will love to read

## BOOK OF LOVE
### By: Maria Shaw

Find out with this fun guide to love and friendship. What should I wear on a first date? Is Libra a good match with Aries? How can I find out if someone wants to go out with me. Discover how to get answers to all of your relationship questions with Maria Shaw's Book of Love. Easy to use and fun to read, this unique guide to relationships gives you:
* An astro compatibility guide for each sun sign.
* Quick and easy magical how-to's.
* Palm reading tips and techniques.
* Simple formulas for determining love number compatibility.

Rs. 150/-

## SPIRITUAL FITNESS
### By: Nancy Mramor

The simple exercises and techniques presented in Spiritual Fitness are not tied to any specific spiritual tradition and can be practiced by anyone. They are designed to lead you toward greater contentment in all areas of your life:
* Improve your physical, emotional, and mental health
* Free yourself from negative behaviours that block happiness
* Discover how to find lasting inner peace
* Deepen your spiritual awareness

Rs. 95/-

## HOW TO HEAL WITH COLOR
### By: Ted Andrews

How to Heal with Color shows you how to use the vibrational effects of color to heal yourself and others. Learn how to:
* Use colors to balance the chakras
* Determine therapeutic colors by muscle testing
* Apply color therapy through touch, projection, breathing, cloth, water, and candles
* Rid yourself of toxins, negativity, and patterns that hinder your life process
* Use the powerful color-healing system of the mystical Qabala to balance and open the psychic centers
* Perform long-distance healing on others

For vibrant physical, emotional, mental, and spiritual health—add color to your life.

Rs. 95/-

## THE INSTINCT TO HEAL
### By: David Servan-Schreiber

Heal is a powerful word. Isn't it presumptuous for a physician to use such a word in the title of a book on stress, anxiety, and depression? I've thought a lot about this question. To me, "healing" means that patients are no longer suffering from the symptoms that they complained of when they first consulted, and that these symptoms do not come back after the treatment has been completed. This is what happens when we treat an infection with antibiotics. The ideas presented in this book are largely inspired by the works of physicians and researchers.

Rs. 195/-

---

### ◉ Fusion Books

X-30, Okhla Industrial Area, Phase-II, New Delhi-110020, Ph.: 41611861, Fax: 41611861.
E-mail: sales@diamondpublication.com, Website: www.diamondpublication.com